95 Phonics Booster Bundle

Summer School Edition

Rising 1st Grade

Teacher Edition

475 Half Day Road, Suite 350
Lincolnshire, IL 60069
847-499-8200
www.95percentgroup.com

Written and published by
95 Percent Group Inc.
Susan L. Hall, EdD, Founder and Chief Executive Officer
475 Half Day Road, Suite 350
Lincolnshire, IL 60069
www.95percentgroup.com

Table of Contents

Introduction

Lessons

Introduction

Description of *95 Phonics Booster Bundle*™: *Summer School Edition* (SSE)

The *95 Phonics Booster Bundle*™: *Summer School Edition* (SSE) is a phonics strand taught in summer school with the whole class or in small groups. An additional use of the program is to teach part or all of the first 25 days in the fall to jump-start the transition to the next school year. This will help ensure that students have mastered the prior year's skills.

This program is consistent with a core value of 95 Percent Group, which is that reading instruction should be teacher directed. Although digital tools are included, this program is grounded in the belief that the teacher—not a computer—teaches students how to read. The 25 daily lessons in this program are designed to teach for 30–45 minutes daily during summer school or as a review at the beginning of the school year. This program serves as a phonics and word study strand and is not intended to be a comprehensive literacy curriculum; it doesn't include read-alouds, oral language and vocabulary development, reading of authentic text, comprehension instruction, and process writing.

By varying the number of practice opportunities provided to students, teachers can manage the lesson time to 30–45 minutes to fit into a summer school schedule. For example, if less time is available, teachers can dictate 1–2 of the 3 sentences provided in the Write Sentences section or have students complete 1 row of Word Completion with Pictures.

Rationale for Developing the *Summer School Edition*

Clients have often asked 95 Percent Group to consider developing a Tier 1 phonics program. Across the company's history, this has been the single most requested new product. The impetus for this request is the large, measurable gains occurring among the students receiving instruction with 95 Percent Group's intervention materials. Having experienced what explicit, systematic, and sequential phonics instruction looks like, clients realize that their core program lacks phonics instruction grounded in the science of reading and the principles of structured literacy. Although a handful of clients have successfully used the intervention routines within their core reading block, most clients have experienced challenges adapting our phonics intervention materials for whole-class use.

Based on client feedback, this program addresses the following needs:

- Inadequate phonics instruction in many popular literacy curricula
- An excessive number of students identified for Tier 2 or 3 phonics intervention
- Inadequate teacher knowledge about the science of reading and effective phonics instruction
- Gaps in students' phonics skill development resulting from school closures, summer breaks, etc.
- A curriculum that enables a seamless transition between in-class and remote learning without disrupting or watering down the instruction
- Digital tools to enhance instruction in any setting

Using the deep phonics expertise of our team as well as leveraging instructional strategies found in our existing phonics products, this new *Summer School Edition* phonics program was not only developed quickly but also entirely by our educator employees. A hallmark of the curriculum is that it provides explicit routines in each of the important components of phonics instruction, including word sorting, sound-spelling mapping with and without phonics chips, word chains, and transfer to text. This program aligns with all of 95 Percent Group's phonics assessments and intervention materials so students will have consistent gestures, chip colors, and routines between Tier 1, summer school, and intervention. New decodable text was written so that passages used in our intervention materials will be fresh for students who require extra support in Tier 2 or 3.

Additionally, to address the potential of school closures, the program was designed to ensure a seamless transition to remote learning without disruption in the curriculum sequence by sending the Student Workbook and manipulatives home. These materials can be used from home in unison with the Presentation files when teachers instruct students on videoconferencing platforms.

How to Use the *Summer School Edition*

Using the *Summer School Edition* is easy because it's an all-inclusive program where teachers receive everything needed for instruction. There is 1 digital component (the Presentation files), which is provided on the company's website at www.95percentgroup.com.

To get started, teachers should read this entire introduction and watch the product training video located online in the Customer Portal (single sign-on). After that, they'll need to cut out the manipulatives and place them in individual student plastic bags (schools will have to provide resealable bags for the letter-sound strips or phonics chips).

A day in the life of a teacher with this program means simply reviewing the lesson ahead of time. Just before instruction begins, teachers turn to the starting page in the TE and display, on a screen, the header page in the Presentation file for that day's lesson. After instructing students to retrieve their individual manipulative bags and workbooks, the teacher spends 30–45 minutes going back and forth between drawing the students' attention to the screen and giving them time to work in their workbooks. Students practice letter formation, fill-in missing letters in CVC words, read and write sentences, read short stories, and respond to the stories through oral prompts.

Materials

There are 2 types of materials included in the Rising 1st Grade SSE program: printed teacher and student materials, and presentation files accessed online at the product's Customer Portal.

Printed Materials Shipped

- **Teacher's Package** – The Teacher's Package includes 1 full-color, spiral-bound TE for Rising 1st grade. Each TE includes 25 days of lessons. The back cover is a firm stock, enabling teachers to hold the book folded back to see a single page with assurance that it will not bend.

- **Student Package** – The Student Package includes 2 components. First, there is a Student Workbook (SW) of approximately 42 pages with full-color covers and grayscale printing on the interior pages. Everything the student needs to participate in the lesson is contained in the workbook. This includes letters with arrows to review letter formation, pictures for identification of initial sounds, high-frequency word boxes to read and build automaticity, designated areas for writing sentences, and text to practice reading sentences and short stories. The second component is the student letter-sound strips. There are 7 strips (containing 3-4 letters each; 26

letters total) printed on durable cardstock that is pulled out from the center of the SW binding. The letter-sound strips support letter-sound association as students trace each letter with their fingers while saying the letter name, keyword, and sound.

Materials Accessed Online at the Customer Portal

- **Presentation Files** – These HTML animated files contain images to guide instruction of the lessons. Teachers access and use the Presentation files on our website either in the classroom or during remote instruction using a videoconferencing platform such as Zoom or Google® Classroom. Because these files are HTML, they are accessible on any device with a current browser, including a Chromebook®.

- **Product Training Video** – This 30-minute training video provides an overview of the program and tips for teaching the lessons. This video is accessible on the Customer Portal by all teachers who have a Teacher's Package. More extensive professional development is available either virtually or in person for an additional fee.

- **Other Teacher Support** – The product's landing page will be updated with teacher support tips and resources as new questions arise. Teachers should check back frequently for additional resources.

Program Components

The *Summer School Edition* is a phonics curriculum that is designed for rising K-2nd grade students and includes the following components:

- Phonological awareness instruction and practice to develop and support phonemic proficiency for efficient word recognition skills
- Letter-sound correspondences
- Letter formation instruction and practice
- Suggestions for developing print concepts while reading text aloud
- Explicit instruction in blending CVC words
- Phonics patterns that are demonstrated and practiced hands-on with phonics chips
- Phoneme-grapheme mapping, including writing letters in sound boxes in the Student Workbook
- High-frequency word practice (based on the Dolch grade-level list)
- Writing words, word chains, sentences, and short responses to passage reading
- Word and phrase fluency practice
- Practice applying phonics knowledge in decodable text specifically written to provide maximum practice for pattern words and to review previously taught patterns
- Instruction in morphological units, including derivational and inflectional suffixes, the most common prefixes and suffixes (based on the work of Marcia K. Henry, author of *Unlocking Literacy* and a consultant to 95 Percent Group in the design of our vocabulary product, *Vocabulary Surge*)
- Instruction and practice in the use of standards-based comprehension processes through oral discussions and written responses after students read decodable texts

Student Engagement

Student engagement is critically important for learning. Stanislas Dehaene's books *Reading in the Brain* and *How We Learn* provide research on the importance of not only holding students' attention but also helping to direct their attention to what's important to learn. He states in *How We Learn* (2020) that research in cognitive science shows that attention is the mechanism used by the brain to select information, amplify it, channel it, and deepen the processing of it. He reports on research that shows that whatever the learner pays attention to causes a strong surge of neural firings, exactly what the synapses need to change their strength and cause learning to happen. In the *Summer School Edition*, multiple techniques are used—such as pointing a finger at vowels in the phonics pattern—to focus the learner's attention on what matters.

In the lesson design of the *Summer School Edition*, there are many techniques to not only engage students but also to focus their attention on key visual information that will facilitate automaticity in the recognition and reading of phonics patterns. It's not possible to learn words individually because there are too many in the English language. The approach in the *Summer School Edition* is to teach the pattern, enabling students to generalize to other words with the same pattern.

Here are some of the ways that the instructional routines in the *Summer School Edition* engage and guide students' attention to what is important to learn:

- Tracing letters to learn letter formation while repeating the letter name, sound, and keyword
- Finding the vowels by pointing to them
- Using gestures (V-shape, closed fist, open fist, etc.) for syllable types so all students are responding during whole-class instruction
- Using hands-on phonics chip movement to amplify learning phonemic awareness to an automatic level
- Writing words in a word chain to see the difference in spellings (e.g., rip, ripe, ride, rid)
- Analyzing how words change meaning by writing the prefixes in small boxes surrounding the Latin root or Anglo-Saxon base word

Each lesson includes student engagement because it's not only critical for learning but also provides the opportunity for corrective feedback.

Alignment with the Science of Reading

The *Summer School Edition* is **research based**. It was developed using the same research base that provided the foundation for *Phonics Lesson Library™* and *Phonics Chip Kits™*, developed by 95 Percent Group in 2014–2016 and 2012 respectively. The studies included in the National Reading Panel report were the initial basis of the design for the *Summer School Edition*, which was confirmed by more recent research studies cited in David Kilpatrick's 2015 book, *Essentials of Assessing, Preventing, and Overcoming Reading Difficulties*. Several fundamental research findings that 95 Percent Group used as guiding principles are shown on the next page.

- Phonics instruction that is <u>systematic</u> is better than no preplanned order of skill instruction.
- Effective phonics instruction follows a <u>prescribed sequence</u> that progresses from simple to complex. Our phonics products follow a skills progression that is defined by 95 Percent Group's phonics continuum so that each lesson builds on earlier mastered concepts.

- Explicit instruction produces the best results. 95 Percent Group's phonics products use an explicit approach where students are directly told the phonics concept. The phonics pattern is emphasized and made more explicit in several ways:
  - By using manipulatives (letter-sound strips and colored chips)
  - By using gestures for the syllable types
  - By reinforcing learning with the reading-writing connection through word chaining, writing words in sound boxes, and writing sentences from dictation
- <u>Orthographic mapping</u> is the process the brain uses to recognize words that are stored in memory. The program supports the importance of orthographic mapping to word learning in several places. First, students identify individual phonemes by moving color-coded sound chips into sound boxes (called Elkonin boxes). Next, our product directs students' attention to the sound-spelling patterns through color-coded sound chips. After mapping the sounds in words, students write letters below, which is the phoneme-grapheme mapping process. David Kilpatrick's book *Essentials of Assessing, Preventing, and Overcoming Reading Difficulties* was released in 2015; the research cited is what was used in the design of the *Summer School Edition*.

Specific, cited research that supports our product design includes:

- *Report of the National Reading Panel: Teaching Children to Read. Report of Subgroups* (2001).
  - "Findings provided solid support for the conclusion that <u>systematic phonics instruction makes a more significant contribution to children's growth in reading than do alternative programs providing unsystematic or no phonics instruction</u>" (p. 2-132).
  - "Phonics instruction has also been <u>widely regarded as particularly beneficial</u> to children with reading problems (e.g., Foorman et al., 1998)" (p. 2-105).

- *Report of the National Reading Panel: Teaching Children to Read Summary Report* (2002).
  - "The meta-analysis revealed that <u>systematic phonics instruction</u> produces significant benefits for students in kindergarten through 6th grade and for children having difficulty learning to read" (p. 9).
  - "First graders who were taught phonics systematically were better able to decode and spell, and they showed significant improvement in their ability to comprehend text" (p. 9).
  - "Across all grade levels, systematic phonics instruction improved the ability of good readers to spell" (p. 10).

- Kilpatrick, D. (2015). *Essentials of Assessing, Preventing, and Overcoming Reading Difficulties*.
  - "<u>Systematic instruction</u> means that the teacher has a specific plan or sequence for introducing letter-sound relationships" (p. 268).
  - "Because the <u>explicit and systematic approach</u> is more successful with most students, the terms *explicit* and *systematic* are often used to distinguish more effective approaches to phonics instruction from less effective ones" (p. 268).
  - "<u>Orthographic memory</u> involves a connection-forming process in which the oral phonemes are 'bonded' to the letters used to represent those phonemes. The phoneme sequence of the word is already established in long-term memory and acts as the anchor for the written sequence of letters used to represent that phonemic sequence" (p. 101).
  - "<u>Orthographic mapping</u> establishes a stable memory of spelling patterns" (p. 81).

In regards to **evidence based**, the *Summer School Edition* has not been the subject of an efficacy study because it is new. However, there are two considerations. First, 95 Percent Group plans to conduct an evidence study upon the program's release. Second, the phonics products upon which the *Summer School Edition* is based have been studied and evaluated in evidence studies—and there is much evidence of their success. For more information, please visit our product landing page, which will be updated once evidence studies are completed.

A discussion about the important components of a phonics program is outlined below.

Phonological Awareness (PA)

Because of the importance of PA in learning to read, the *Summer School Edition* includes a short warm-up of PA at the start of each lesson and a PA wrap-up at the end of the lesson. As the lessons progress, the PA prompts increase in complexity from blending and substituting syllables in words, segmenting 2-3 phonemes, to finally substituting the initial sound in a word.

Orthographic Mapping

One of the most important new insights from the past 5 years is that instructing students to study letter strings is more effective than using cues such as context or initial letter to figure out an unknown word. The process of going from speech to print is critical in developing an image of the letter strings in a word. The *Summer School Edition* explicitly teaches the link between the phonemic sounds in a word and the letter or letters that spell each sound. 95 Percent Group developed an approach where specific colored chips represent certain types of sounds; this approach was published in 2012 as the *Phonics Chip Kit* and more recently incorporated in the 2020 *95 Phonics Core Program*™. The recent attention to the process of orthographic mapping— mapping letters to sounds—confirms our approach of emphasizing sound-spelling mapping. The *Summer School Edition* (Rising 2nd and Rising 3rd) includes sound-spelling mapping with and without chips in many of the days.

Fluency

Fluency occurs when the reader recognizes nearly all the words in a text. According to Joseph Torgeson (2004), readers achieve fluency when they not only have a sufficient Word Bank of known words but also have the skills to efficiently figure out new words.

To prepare students to fluently read connected text, it's best to support gradual steps to getting there. First, they need fluency at the word level. Then, they need to read phrases. Finally, fluency occurs at the sentence and paragraph levels.

High-Frequency Words (HFWs)

The *Summer School Edition* uses the Dolch list of high-frequency words for kindergarten through grade 2. Students are exposed to the words in sentences, short stories, and passages. Also, students get a chance to increase their automatic recognition of the words through daily fluency practice reading the words. Most of the words become decodable once the skill is taught in the program. For example, the word *did* is included in Dolch's grade K list. The closed syllable pattern with the short vowel i is reviewed in Day 3 of the Rising 1st lesson; after that, the word *did* is no longer considered a HFW because it is now decodable by the pattern that has been taught.

Letter-Sound Correspondence

The *Summer School Edition*'s Rising 1st-grade curriculum includes 5 days of letter-sound review. The *Summer School Edition* front-loads letter-sound review so students can jump right into the application of this foundational skill. Once students have mastery of letter-sound association, they can begin the process of blending the sounds to read simple CVC words, moving into reading and writing simple sentences, and then putting it all together in short decodable stories.

Although the explicit review of letter-sound correspondence ends after Day 5 in the *Summer School Edition*, the routine established with the letter-sound strips allows for additional distributed practice, as needed, throughout the remaining days of the program.

Alignment of the *95 Phonics Booster Bundle Summer School Edition* with 95 Percent Group's Core and Intervention Materials

The compatibility of 95 Percent Group's summer school phonics program with our newly created core and well-established interventions is seamless. The *Summer School Edition* is intentionally designed to align with all our other phonics products in the following ways:

- All our phonics products (*Phonics Lesson Library*, *Phonics Chip Kits*, and *95 Phonics Core Program*) are aligned to the same phonics continuum and the same scope and sequence.
- Because the skills in the *Summer School Edition* are taught in the same sequence as our intervention programs, placement in intervention is straightforward. If a student doesn't master a skill with Tier 1 instruction, the teacher will know immediately where to start intervention in Tier 2 or 3.
- The phonics chip colors are the same in core, summer school, and small-group intervention instruction; it is preferable for students who struggle not to switch colors or approaches between what they hear in whole-class and small-group instruction.
- The syllable gestures are the same between core, summer school, and intervention (e.g., closed fist for closed syllables, V-shaped fingers for the silent-e syllable, etc.).
- The key instructional routines are taught the same way in Tier 1 and intervention (for example, in a word chain, the students are asked which sound changes before being asked which letter changes). Students will have learned the routines in the *Summer School Edition* and this should accelerate progress in small-group interventions.
- The decodable text for the *Summer School Edition* has been written specifically for each lesson; therefore students who need intervention will be exposed to text that is new to them, so they won't have memorized it and must use their pattern-recognition skills to read unfamiliar words.

When schools use different Tier 1 and intervention programs, struggling students often fail to generalize and transfer skills because of misalignment in instructional practices between the programs. Students spend too much attention trying to switch back and forth in routines, colors, procedures, and techniques as they transition from Tier 1 to intervention. By using a summer school program with the same structured literacy processes as the 95 Percent Group core and intervention materials, students who receive instruction in summer school benefit from the crossover of processes, strategies, and instructional language. In fact, implementing a strong, comprehensive summer school phonics program that is explicit, sequential, and cumulative should reduce the need for intervention for a percentage of students during the traditional school year.

　　

Scope and Sequence

The scope and sequence for the *Summer School Edition* is available for download on the product's landing page in the Customer Portal.

Overview of Lesson Structure

The lessons in the Rising 1st-grade *Summer School Edition* include the following sections with the exception of the first 5 days which review letter-sound correspondence and letter formation:

- **Concepts of Print** – On Day 3, students review the differences between letters, words, and sentences. Also, the importance of uppercase letters at the beginning of a sentence and punctuation at the end.
- **Phonological Awareness** – Each day starts and ends with a warm-up or wrap-up.
- **Letter-Sound Correspondence** – Using a pointer finger, students trace a letter on a letter-sound strip that contains either 3 or 4 pairs of lowercase and uppercase letters and associated keywords. By referencing this letter-sound support during a lesson, students can use the keywords to retrieve each letter's sound.
- **Letter Formation** – Handwriting of lowercase and uppercase letters is explicitly reviewed through the teacher modeling letter formation with stroke talk. Students follow arrows to trace letters with a finger and pencil on solid lines followed by tracing letters on dotted lines. Practice on each new letter is supported in the workbook on writing paper with solid toplines and bottom lines and dotted midlines. The program uses a ball-and-stick font that is aligned with the Zaner-Bloser Handwriting© approach.
- **Reading** – After reviewing 3 consonants and the first short vowel (/ă/), teachers provide an explicit review on how to blend sounds into words on Day 2. Students practice with the teacher and begin reading words independently at the end of Day 4. Students are reading short stories soon after that.
- **Writing** – Because of the strong reading-writing connection, students start writing a letter for a picture's initial sound in Day 1. Writing sentences begins on Day 6.
- **High-Frequency Words (HFWs)** – Instruction is provided on 4 high-frequency words each day based on the Dolch pre-primer and primer lists. Teachers finger-stretch the sounds and show and discuss the spelling of each new word as well as use it in a sentence.

English Learners and Students on IEPs for Reading

English Learners

English Learners (ELs) often need instruction in the phonological structure of a new language, especially when those structures differ from their native language. For example, Spanish-speaking students often need support to help them move from the syllabic structure of their native language to the phonemic structure of English. This instruction can be good for all English Learners. Those with strength in the phonological structure of their native language will pick up the new language fairly quickly with some instruction. Those with a deficit in their native language will require more explicit instruction. Clients have provided evidence to us that their ELs benefit from and make excellent progress with our materials because the instructional routines provide explicit information about the structure of the English language. Additionally, the embedded routines allow students to move through advanced levels more quickly, preparing them for higher levels of orthographic mapping.

Students on IEPs for Reading Disabilities

Through the continuous teacher–student interaction of the gradual release model, teachers are able to differentiate and scaffold as necessary. This allows teachers to spend as much—or as little—time as necessary on a given skill. Moving students forward as quickly as we can, but as slowly as we must, is key to effective intervention instruction.

In order to provide differentiated instruction for students who are struggling, all of the lessons in the *Summer School Edition*, as well as in the *Phonics Lesson Library, Phonics Chip Kit*, and *95 Phonics Core Program*, have the I DO, WE DO, YOU DO modeling cycle. This cycle provides a gradual release from teacher modeling to students successfully doing the task independently.

All the phonics programs from 95 Percent Group, including the *Summer School Edition*, use manipulatives in instruction. Manipulatives are useful, especially in providing support for students who struggle to learn the skills. All the senses are used in these multisensory lessons. Some examples are:

- Visual – Students see the letters.
- Auditory – Students hear the teacher segmenting the words into individual sounds.
- Kinesthetic – Students make gestures and move their pencils when writing letters in the sound boxes.
- Tactile – Students feel the pencil as they write on paper.

During the I DO and WE DO portions of the lesson, the visual and auditory sensory pathways of students are engaged simultaneously though teacher modeling and presentation with manipulatives such as sound chips, Elkonin boxes, word cards, and decodable texts. The WE DO portion of the lesson engages visual, auditory, and kinesthetic senses.

Reference List

- Dehaene, S. (2017). Reading in the brain: The science and evolution of a human invention. New York, NY: Viking.
- Dehaene, S. (2020). How we learn: Why brains learn better than any machine…for now. New York, NY: Viking.
- Dolch Word. (n.d.). Dolch word list by grade (frequency). http://www.dolchword.net/dolch-word-list-frequency-grade.html
- Eunice Kennedy Shriver National Institute of Child Health and Human Development, NIH, DHHS. (2000). Report of the National Reading Panel: Teaching children to read: Reports of the subgroups (00-4754). Washington, DC: U.S. Government Printing Office.
- Farrell, L., Hunter, M., & Osenga, T. (2019). A new model for teaching high-frequency words. WETA Reading Rockets. https://www.readingrockets.org/article/new-model-teaching-high-frequency-words. Downloaded 6-8-2020.
- Henry, M. (2010). Unlocking literacy: Effective decoding & spelling instruction (2nd ed.). Baltimore, MD: Paul H. Brookes.
- Kilpatrick, D. A. (2015). Essentials of assessing, preventing, and overcoming reading difficulties. Hoboken, NJ: John Wiley & Sons.
- Kilpatrick, D. A. (2016). Equipped for reading success: A comprehensive, step by step program for developing phonemic awareness and fluent word recognition. Syracuse, NY: Casey & Kirsch Publishers.
- *Seidenberg, M. (2017). Language at the speed of sight: How we read, why so many can't, and what can be done about it. New York, NY: Basic Books.*
- Torgesen, J. K. (2004). Avoiding the devastating downward spiral: The evidence that early intervention prevents reading failure. American Educator, 28(3), 6–19.
- WISE Channel. (2013, October 25). How the brain learns to read - Prof. Stanislas Dehaene [Video file]. Retrieved from https://www.youtube.com/watch?v=25GI3-kiLdo

Day 1

Days 1–5: Letter-Sound Correspondence & Letter Formation

Learning Objective

Students demonstrate understanding of all 26 letters by correctly identifying and writing the uppercase and lowercase as well as associating the correct sound with the letter.

DAY 1 — Letters Tt, Pp, Nn, Aa

Phonological Awareness Warm-Up

PHONOLOGICAL AWARENESS: SYLLABLES

Today we are going to practice saying a word and then <u>changing a syllable</u> to make a new word. Listen carefully. Sometimes we will change the first syllable, and other times we'll change the last syllable.

Let's practice 2 words together.
- Say seashell: (seashell) Change /shell/ to /shore/. Word? seashore
- Say upstairs: (upstairs) Change /up/ to /down/. Word? downstairs

Now it's your turn. Here are the instructions:
- I'll say a word and you repeat it.
- Next, I'll tell you a syllable to change.
- Then, tell me the new word. Ready?

Say haircut: (haircut) Change /cut/ to /brush/. Word?	hairbrush
Say raincoat: (raincoat) Change /coat/ to /drop/. Word?	raindrop
Say toolbox: (toolbox) Change /tool/ to /shoe/. Word?	shoebox
Say washcloth: (washcloth) Change /wash/ to /dish/. Word?	dishcloth
Say airport: (airport) Change /port/ to /plane/. Word?	airplane
Say eyeball: (eyeball) Change /ball/ to /lid/. Word?	eyelid
Say goldfish: (goldfish) Change /gold/ to /blue/. Word?	bluefish
Say dustpan: (dustpan) Change /pan/ to /cloth/. Word?	dustcloth
Say farmhouse: (farmhouse) Change /farm/ to /bird/. Word?	birdhouse
Say carport: (carport) Change /port/ to /load/. Word?	carload
Say footprint: (footprint) Change /print/ to /ball/. Word?	football
Say herself: (herself) Change /her/ to /him/. Word?	himself
Say raindrop: (raindrop) Change /drop/ to /bow/. Word?	rainbow
Say football: (football) Change /foot/ to /base/. Word?	baseball
Say sandbox: (sandbox) Change /sand/ to /mail/. Word?	mailbox
Say sunlight: (sunlight) Change /light/ to /roof/. Word?	sunroof

Letter-Sound Correspondence

REVIEW OF LETTER-SOUNDS: Tt - /t/, Pp - /p/, Nn - /n/, AND Aa - /ă/

Today we will practice the letter names and sounds of 4 letters: Tt, Pp, Nn, and Aa.

There are 2 ways to write each of these letters. We use an uppercase letter to spell the first sound in a name or a special place. We also use an uppercase letter to begin a sentence. We use a lowercase letter all other times.

Let's review these 4 letters. Find letter-sound strip #1.

When I say a letter, place your pointer finger on it and say 3 things: the letter name, the keyword, and the sound.

Let's practice one together. Ready? Place your pointer finger on the uppercase T.
- **Letter name?** uppercase T
- **Keyword?** toe
- **Sound?** /t/

(Mix up your prompts so that you're not asking for the uppercase and lowercase letters next to one another. Ask for each letter at least once.)

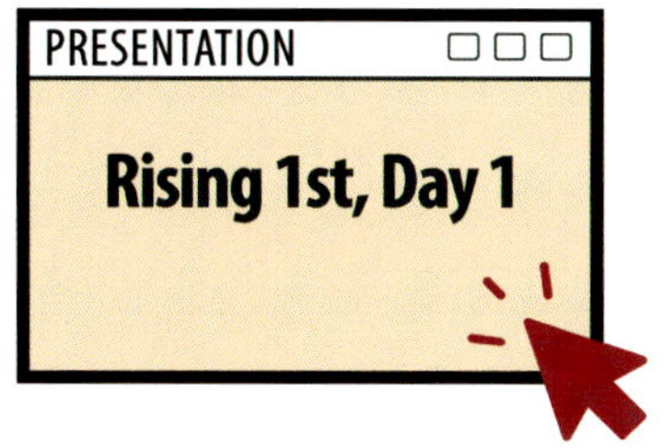

Letter-Sound Correspondence Review			Letter Name?	Keyword?	Sound?
Tt		Uppercase	uppercase T	toe	/t/
		Lowercase	t	toe	/t/
Pp		Uppercase	uppercase P	pig	/p/
		Lowercase	p	pig	/p/
Nn		Uppercase	uppercase N	nest	/n/
		Lowercase	n	nest	/n/
Aa		Uppercase	uppercase A	apple	/ă/
		Lowercase	a	apple	/ă/

INITIAL SOUND PRACTICE

Now we will look at a picture and write the first sound in the word. Let's do the first 2 together.

(Display tent.)
Word? tent
- **First sound?** /t/
- **Letter?** t
- I say /t/ while writing the letter *t*.

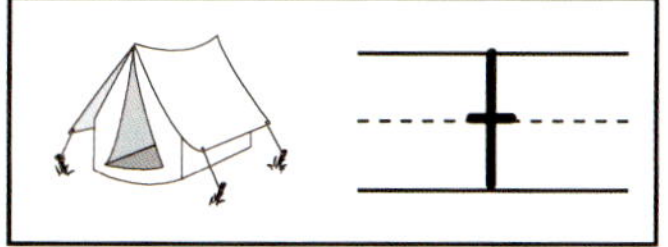

(Display <u>apple</u>.)
Word? apple
- **First sound?** /ă/
- **Letter?** a
- **I say /ă/ while writing the letter** *a*.

Now it's your turn. Turn to page 2 in your Student Workbook.
(Review the name of each picture with students before they begin.
Row 1: ant, nut, pop, tie; Row 2: panda, tire, net, alligator)

Here are the steps:
1. Say the word.
2. Say the first sound in the word.
3. Say the letter.
4. Repeat the sound as you write the letter.

Answer Key

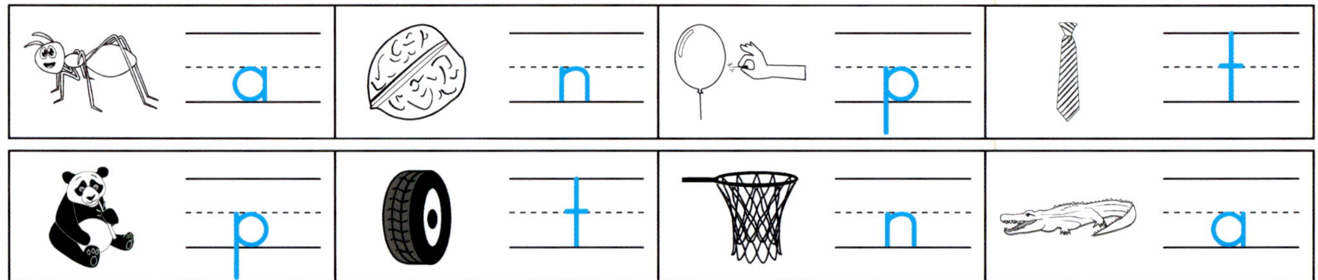

Letter Formation

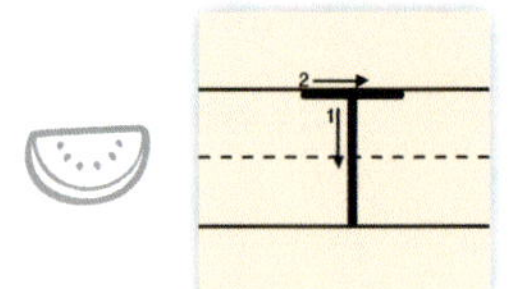

REVIEW OF LETTER FORMATION: Tt, Pp, Nn, AND Aa

We're going to practice writing the 4 uppercase and lowercase letters we have been studying today.

Watch me write <u>uppercase letter *T*</u>.
1. Start at the topline. Pull down straight. Lift.
2. Back to the topline. Slide right.

Now it's your turn. Turn to page 2 in your Student Workbook.
Find the line that has a watermelon slice in front of it. We will
practice writing the uppercase letters first.

Letter name? uppercase T **Sound?** /t/
- **Finger ready? Follow the arrows to trace the letter while saying /t/.**
- **Pencil ready? Follow the arrows to trace the letter while saying /t/.**
- **Pencil ready? Follow the dotted lines to trace the letter while saying /t/. Do this 2 times.**
- **Pencil ready? Write the uppercase T until the line is filled. Don't forget to say /t/ as you write it.**

Note: Since letter formation is a review for students, this program will have students practice uppercase letters first followed by their lowercase counterparts.

(Following the procedure on the previous page, repeat the same process with the uppercase letters in this order: *P*, *N*, and *A*. Reference the stroke talk in the table below.)

Stroke Talk for Review of Uppercase Letter Formation – *P*, *N*, and *A*		
Watch me write uppercase letter ____.		
 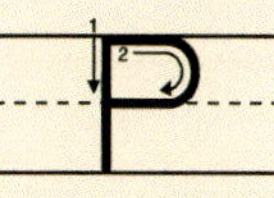	 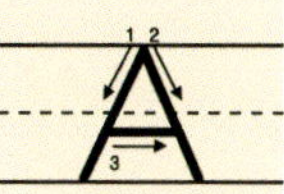	 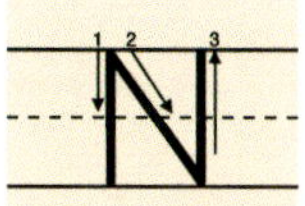
1. **Start at the topline. Pull down straight. Lift.** 2. **Back to the top. Curve forward, slide to the left.**	1. **Start at the topline, pull down straight. Lift.** 2. **Back to the top. Slant to the right.** 3. **Push up to the topline.**	1. **Start at the topline. Slant to the left. Lift.** 2. **Back to the topline. Slant to the right. Lift.** 3. **Slide across the midline.**

 **Now it's your turn. Find the line that has ___ in front of it.**
- **Finger ready? Follow the arrows to trace the letter while saying /_ /.**
- **Pencil ready? Follow the arrows to trace the letter while saying /_ /.**
- **Pencil ready? Follow the dotted lines to trace the letter while saying /_ /. Do this 2 times.**
- **Pencil ready? Write the uppercase ___ until the line is filled. Don't forget to say /_ / as you write it.**

Now let's practice the lowercase letters.
Watch me write the <u>lowercase letter *t*.</u>
1. **Start at the topline. Pull down straight. Lift.**
2. **Back to the midline. Slide right.**

 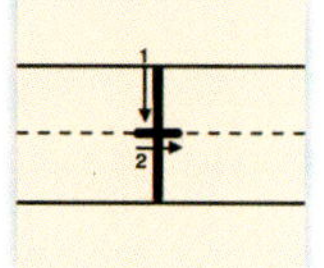

 **Your turn. Look at the top of page 3 in your workbook. Find the line that has a present in front of it.**

Letter name? t Sound? /t/
- **Finger ready? Follow the arrows to trace the letter while saying /t/.**
- **Pencil ready? Follow the arrows to trace the letter while saying /t/.**
- **Pencil ready? Follow the dotted lines to trace the letter while saying /t/. Do this 2 times.**
- **Pencil ready? Write the lowercase t until the line is filled. Don't forget to say /t/ as you write it.**

(Following the procedure on the previous page, repeat the same process with the lowercase letters in this order: *p*, *n*, and *a*. Reference the stroke talk in the table below.)

Stroke Talk for Review of Lowercase Letter Formation – *p*, *n*, and *a*		
Watch me write lowercase letter ____.		
 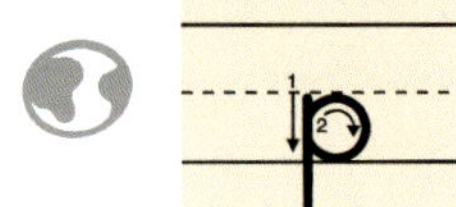	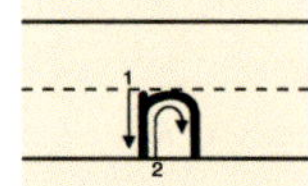 	 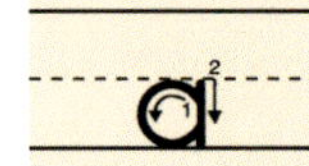
1. Start at the midline. Pull down low. 2. Push up. Circle forward.	1. Start at the midline. Pull down straight. 2. Push up, curve forward, pull down straight.	1. Start at the midline. Circle back and around, push up. 2. Pull down straight.

 Now it's your turn. Find the line that has ___ in front of it.
- Finger ready? Follow the arrows to trace the letter while saying /_ /.
- Pencil ready? Follow the arrows to trace the letter while saying /_ /.
- Pencil ready? Follow the dotted lines to trace the letter while saying /_ /. Do this 2 times.
- Pencil ready? Write the lowercase ___ until the line is filled. Don't forget to say /_ / as you write it.

High-Frequency Words

When you start reading phrases and stories, there may be certain words that are difficult to read by sounding them out. Each day, we will review 4 words so that you can easily read them in stories. Because these words occur often in text, they are called "high-frequency words."

Now I'm going to show you how to read a high-frequency word. Watch me, my turn.

(Display a.)
The word is a (/ā/), as in the sentence "I have a pencil."
- **Watch me finger-stretch the sound. /ā/** (Show thumb for /ā/.)
- **There is 1 sound in the word *a*. This word is spelled with 1 letter, *a*.**

Now it's your turn. Word? a How many letters? 1
The letter name is a. Say it with me. a

a 

(Use the process below to review the next 3 words.)

HFW List	
and /ă/ /n/ /d/	• **The word is ______. What is the word? ______** • **Listen for this word in the following sentence.** (Use the word in a sentence.) • **Watch me finger-stretch the sounds.** • **There are** (number) **sound(s) in the word ______.** • **This word is spelled with** (number) **letter(s), ______.**
I /ī/	**Now it's your turn.** • **Word? ______ How many letter(s)? ______**
the /<u>th</u>/ /ŭ/	• **The letter name(s) are ______. Say them with me. ______**

and
I
the

Note: The letters *th* are underlined (/th/) because the digraph in the word *the* is voiced.

FLUENCY: HIGH-FREQUENCY WORDS

Now we will practice reading the words we have learned.

(Display the high-frequency word grid. Prompt students by saying **"Word?"** at each box.)

the	I	and	a
I	a	the	and
the	I	and	a

Note: Point out that when the letter *I* stands alone as the high-frequency word *I*, it will always be uppercase.

Phonological Awareness Wrap-Up

PHONOLOGICAL AWARENESS: SYLLABLES

Now we will practice saying a word and then <u>changing a syllable</u> to make a new word. Remember to listen carefully. Sometimes we will change the first syllable, and other times we'll change the last syllable.

Let's review the instructions:
- **I'll say a word and you repeat it.**
- **Next, I'll tell you a syllable to change.**
- **Then, tell me the new word. Ready?**

Say sunlight: (sunlight) Change /light/ to /roof/. Word?	sunroof
Say daytime: (daytime) Change /day/ to /night/. Word?	nighttime
Say uptown: (uptown) Change /up/ to /down/. Word?	downtown
Say hometown: (hometown) Change /town/ to /made/. Word?	homemade
Say bookmark: (bookmark) Change /mark/ to /worm/. Word?	bookworm
Say bowtie: (bowtie) Change /bow/ to /neck/. Word?	necktie
Say cookbook: (cookbook) Change /cook/ to /school/. Word?	schoolbook
Say daytime: (daytime) Change /time/ to /dream/. Word?	daydream
Say doorknob: (doorknob) Change /knob/ to /bell/. Word?	doorbell
Say moonlight: (moonlight) Change /moon/ to /sun/. Word?	sunlight
Say cheesecake: (cheesecake) Change /cheese/ to /cup/. Word?	cupcake
Say birdbath: (birdbath) Change /bath/ to /house/. Word?	birdhouse
Say baseball: (baseball) Change /base/ to /soft/. Word?	softball
Say fishpond: (fishpond) Change /pond/ to /bowl/. Word?	fishbowl
Say sailboat: (sailboat) Change /sail/ to /life/. Word?	lifeboat
Say doorbell: (doorbell) Change /bell/ to /stop/. Word?	doorstop

DAY 2   Letters Mm, Dd, Gg

Phonological Awareness Warm-Up

PHONOLOGICAL AWARENESS: SYLLABLES

Today we are going to learn how to <u>blend syllables</u> in words that are not compound words. In the Day 1 lesson, the words we worked with were compound words where there were 2 words you know like in air-plane and cow-girl. In this lesson, the word parts, or syllables, aren't words but when we blend the 2 syllables, they will make a word you know.

Listen and watch while I show you the first word.

(Display <u>table</u> in the top box.)

- **I'll say the parts slowly while pulling a rectangle down for each syllable.**
- **The first syllable is <u>ta</u>. The last syllable is <u>ble</u>.**
- **Now I say the syllables together while sliding my finger along the line.** (Pretend to slide finger.) **table**

Let's try one together. (Display <u>baby</u> in the top box.)
- **Say it slowly while I pull down a rectangle for each syllable.**
- **Say the first syllable with me. ba Say the last syllable with me. by**
- **Now say the syllables together while I slide my finger along the line.** (Pretend to slide finger.) **baby**

Now we'll blend syllables without pictures, rectangles, or lines. Here are the instructions:
- **I'll say the first syllable and you repeat it.**
- **Next, I'll say the last syllable and you repeat it.**
- **Then, tell me the word. Ready?**

Note: Throughout this lesson, glance at the word before saying the prompt so you'll know how to pronounce each syllable.

Note: Although the rectangles in the Presentation file are animated, pretend to pull them down to model for students. To increase engagement, have the students pretend to pull them down on the "We do" example.

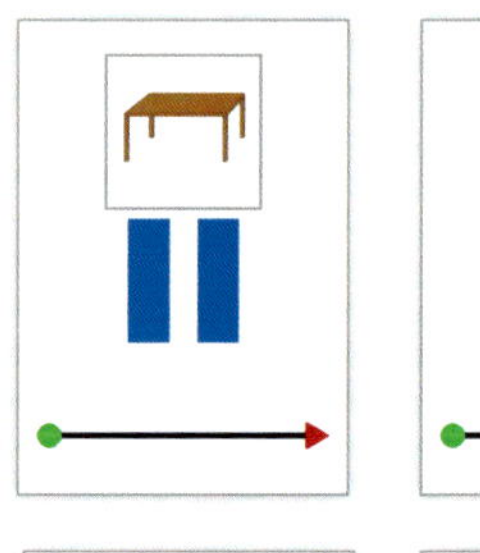
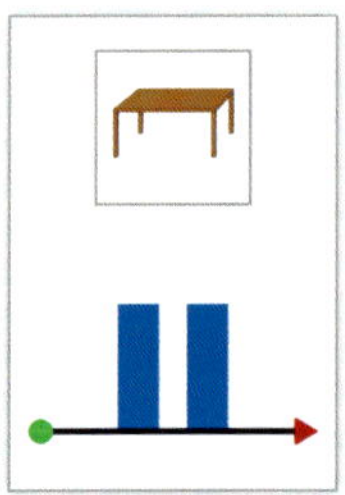
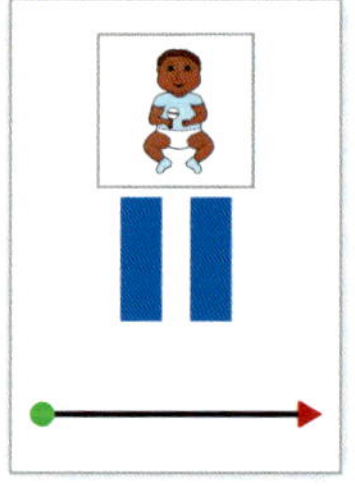
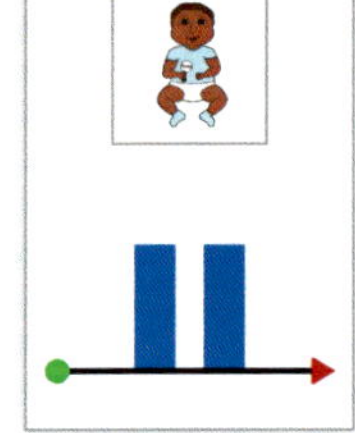

Say mu: (mu) Say sic: (sic) Word?	music	Say nap: (nap) Say kin: (kin) Word?	napkin
Say pa: (pa) Say per: (per) Word?	paper	Say win: (win) Say ter: (ter) Word?	winter
Say thun: (thun) Say der: (der) Word?	thunder	Say tea: (tea) Say cher: (cher) Word?	teacher
Say pen: (pen) Say cil: (cil) Word?	pencil	Say bas: (bas) Say ket: (ket) Word?	basket
Say sis: (sis) Say ter: (ter) Word?	sister	Say bro: (bro) Say ken: (ken) Word?	broken
Say pump: (pump) Say kin: (kin) Word?	pumpkin	Say up: (up) Say set: (set) Word?	upset
Say han: (han) Say dle: (dle) Word?	handle	Say sim: (sim) Say ple: (ple) Word?	simple
Say win: (win) Say dow: (dow) Word?	window	Say pic: (pic) Say nic: (nic) Word?	picnic

Day
2

Letter-Sound Correspondence

REVIEW OF LETTER-SOUNDS: Mm - /m/, Dd - /d/, AND Gg - /g/

Today we will practice the letter names and sounds of 3 letters: Mm, Dd, and Gg.

There are 2 ways to write each of these letters. Remember, we use an uppercase letter to spell the first sound in a name or a special place. We also use an uppercase letter to begin a sentence. We use a lowercase letter all other times.

Let's review these 3 letters. Find letter-sound strip #2.

When I say a letter, place your pointer finger on it and say 3 things: the letter name, the keyword, and the sound.

Let's practice one together. Ready? Place your pointer finger on the uppercase M.

- **Letter name?** uppercase M
- **Keyword?** mouse
- **Sound?** /m/

(Mix up your prompts so that you're not asking for the uppercase and lowercase letters next to one another. Ask for each letter at least once.)

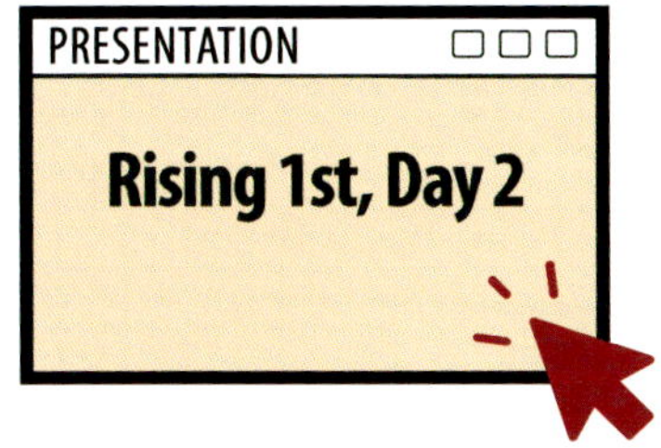

Letter-Sound Correspondence Review					
			Letter Name?	Keyword?	Sound?
Mm		Uppercase	uppercase M	mouse	/m/
		Lowercase	m	mouse	/m/
Dd		Uppercase	uppercase D	dog	/d/
		Lowercase	d	dog	/d/
Gg		Uppercase	uppercase G	goat	/g/
		Lowercase	g	goat	/g/

INITIAL SOUND PRACTICE

Now we will look at a picture and write the first sound in the word. Let's do the first one together.

(Display mad.)
Word? mad
- **First sound?** /m/
- **Letter?** m
- I say /m/ while writing the letter *m*.

Now it's your turn. Turn to page 3 in your Student Workbook. (Review the name of each picture with students before they begin. Row 1: nickel, tent, pig, map; Row 2: dot, girl, mask, astronaut)

Here are the steps:
1. Say the word.
2. Say the first sound in the word.
3. Say the letter.
4. Repeat the sound as you write the letter.

Answer Key

Letter Formation

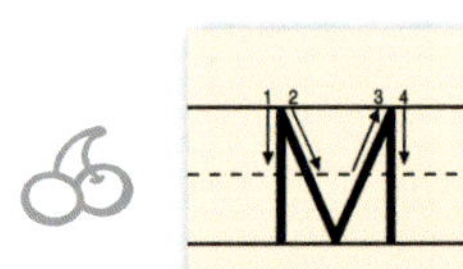

REVIEW LETTER FORMATION: Mm, Dd, AND Gg

We're going to practice writing the 3 uppercase and lowercase letters we have been studying today.

Watch me write uppercase letter *M*.
1. Start at the topline, pull down straight. Lift.
2. Back to the topline, slant right.
3. Slant up.
4. Pull down straight.

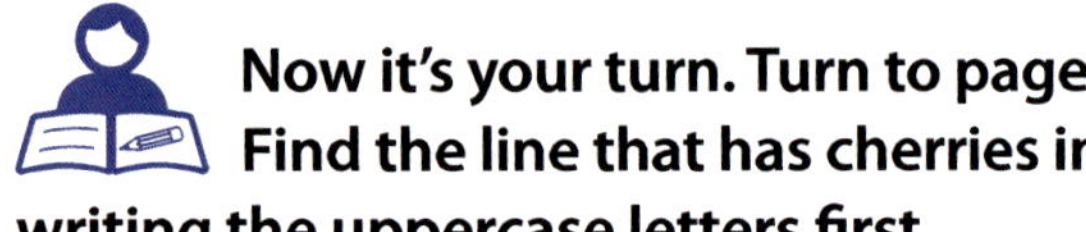

Now it's your turn. Turn to page 4 in your Student Workbook. Find the line that has cherries in front of it. We will practice writing the uppercase letters first.

Letter name? uppercase M Sound? /m/
- Finger ready? Follow the arrows to trace the letter while saying /m/.
- Pencil ready? Follow the arrows to trace the letter while saying /m/.
- Pencil ready? Follow the dotted lines to trace the letter while saying /m/. Do this 2 times.
- Pencil ready? Write the uppercase M until the line is filled. Don't forget to say /m/ as you write it.

Day
2

(Following the procedure on the previous page, repeat the same process with the uppercase letters in this order: D and G. Reference the stroke talk in the table below.)

Stroke Talk for Review of Uppercase Letter Formation – *D* and *G*	
Watch me write uppercase letter _____.	

1. Start at the topline. Pull down straight. Lift. 2. Back to the topline. Curve forward, slide along the bottom line.	1. Start near the topline. Circle back. Pull along the bottom line, push up. 2. Slide to the left.

 Now it's your turn. Find the line that has ___ in front of it.
- **Finger ready? Follow the arrows to trace the letter while saying /_ /.**
- **Pencil ready? Follow the arrows to trace the letter while saying /_ /.**
- **Pencil ready? Follow the dotted lines to trace the letter while saying /_ /. Do this 2 times.**
- **Pencil ready? Write the uppercase ___ until the line is filled. Don't forget to say /_ / as you write it.**

Now let's practice the lowercase letters.
Watch me write the lowercase letter *m*.
1. **Start at the midline, pull down straight.**
2. **Push up, curve forward, pull down straight.**
3. **Push up, curve forward, pull down straight.**

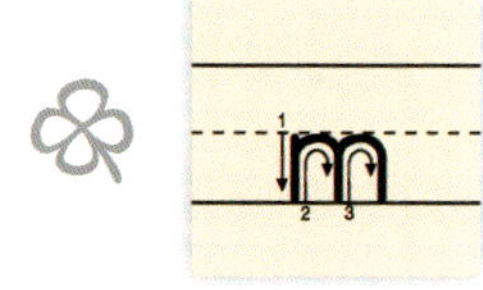

Your turn. You should still be on page 4 of your workbook. Find the line that has a 4-leaf clover in front of it.

Letter name? m Sound? /m/
- **Finger ready? Follow the arrows to trace the letter while saying /m/.**
- **Pencil ready? Follow the arrows to trace the letter while saying /m/.**
- **Pencil ready? Follow the dotted lines to trace the letter while saying /m/. Do this 2 times.**
- **Pencil ready? Write the lowercase m until the line is filled. Don't forget to say /m/ as you write it.**

(Following the procedure on the previous page, repeat the same process with the lowercase letters in this order: d and g. Reference the stroke talk in the table below.)

Stroke Talk for Review of Lowercase Letter Formation – *d* and *g*	
Watch me write lowercase letter ____.	
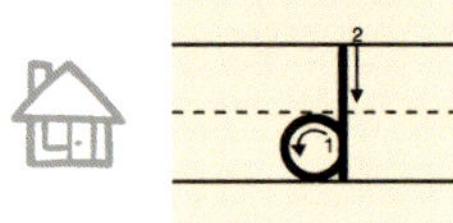	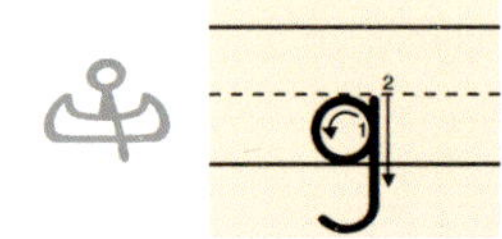
1. Start at the midline, circle back and around, push up. 2. Pull down straight.	1. Start at the midline, circle back and around, push up. 2. Pull down low. Curve left. Stop.

 Now it's your turn. Find the line that has ___ in front of it.
- **Finger ready? Follow the arrows to trace the letter while saying /__/.**
- **Pencil ready? Follow the arrows to trace the letter while saying /__/.**
- **Pencil ready? Follow the dotted lines to trace the letter while saying /__/. Do this 2 times.**
- **Pencil ready? Write the lowercase ___ until the line is filled. Don't forget to say /__/ as you write it.**

Reading

BLENDING AWARENESS

We have been reviewing some of the sounds in words. Today you will learn how to blend sounds together so that there is no space between them. The 6 consonant sounds you've reviewed so far are /t/, /p/, /n/, /m/, /d/, and /g/. You have reviewed 1 vowel sound, /ă/.

When reading words, there are no pauses between the sounds. I'll use these colored chips to represent the sounds in words. The blue chips represent consonant sounds, and the red chip represents a short vowel sound. The short vowel sound you've already learned is /ă/.

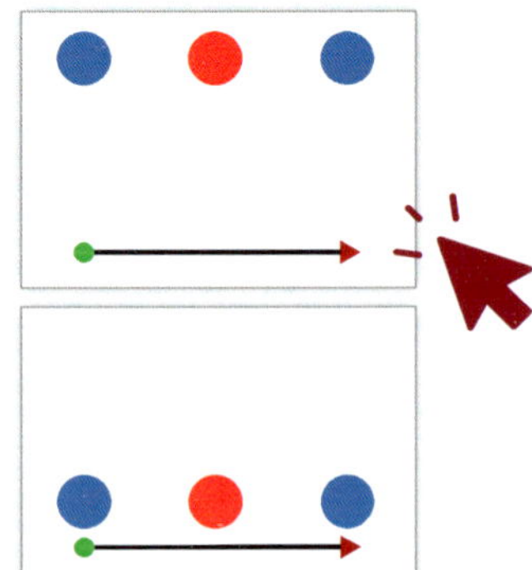

Watch me, my turn. (Chip movement is animated on the Presentation file.)
- **The word is spelled <u>m-a-n</u>.**
- **The first sound is /m/, which I'll say while pulling a blue chip down.**
- **The next sound is /ă/, which I'll say while pulling a red chip down.**
- **The last sound is /n/, which I'll say while pulling a blue chip down.**

Note: In the following steps, advance the Presentation file by clicking with each sound you say. On the second and third times, the chips will move closer; mirror this by reducing the length of the pauses between sounds.

- **Watch me point to each chip while saying the sounds again.**
  (The 3 dots indicate pausing 3 seconds between sounds.)
  /mmm/…/ăăă/…/nnn/

- **Watch a second time. The chips move closer together as I say the sounds closer together.** (Pause 2 seconds between sounds.) **/mm/../ăă/../nn/**
- **Now, we'll see the chips move even closer together this third time. When the chips are closer together, there are shorter pauses between sounds.** (Pause 1 second between sounds.) **/m/./ă/./n/**
- **I'll push the chips together so that they are touching.**
- **Finally, notice that there is NO space between the chips and I'm not pausing between sounds. I hold each sound until my mouth moves into the next sound. With no pauses between sounds, I pronounce the word** *man.*

(Repeat the procedure with the words in the word list in the right margin.)

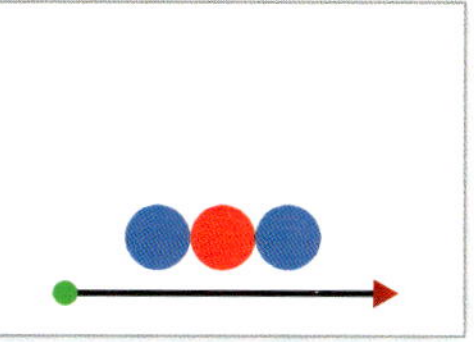

1. am	5. nag
2. nap	6. map
3. at	7. an
4. mad	8. mat

High-Frequency Words

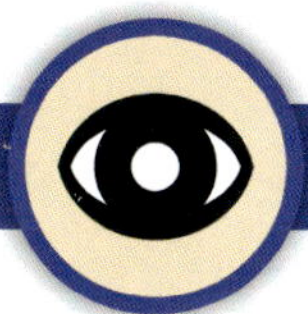

Now I'm going to show you how to read 4 more high-frequency words. Watch me, my turn.

(Display do.)
The word is do, as in the sentence "Do you like tacos?"
- **Watch me finger-stretch the sounds. /d/ /ū/** (Show thumb for /d/ and pointer finger for /ū/.)
- **There are 2 sounds in the word** *do.* **This word is spelled with 2 letters,** *d-o.*

Now it's your turn. Word? do How many letters? 2
The letter names are d-o. Say them with me. d-o

(Use the process below to review the next 3 words.)

do

HFW List	
see /s/ /ē/	• **The word is _______. What is the word? _______** • **Listen for this word in the following sentence.** (Use the word in a sentence.) • **Watch me finger-stretch the sounds.** • **There are** (number) **sound(s) in the word _______.** • **This word is spelled with** (number) **letter(s), _______.**
to /t/ /ū/	**Now it's your turn.** • **Word? _______ How many letter(s)? _______** • **The letter name(s) are _______. Say them with me. _______**
you /y/ /ū/	

see
to
you

FLUENCY: HIGH-FREQUENCY WORDS

Now we will practice reading the words we know.

(Display the high-frequency word grid. Prompt students by saying **"Word?"** at each box.)

see	to	you	do
I	the	see	and
do	a	to	you

Day 2

Phonological Awareness Wrap-Up

PHONOLOGICAL AWARENESS: SYLLABLES

Let's practice <u>blending syllables</u> to make a word.

I'll do the first one.
- I say <u>mon</u>. I say <u>key</u>.
- Now I put them together to make a word: mon-key, monkey.

We will practice 2 together.
- Say <u>tur</u>: (tur) Say <u>key</u>: (key) Word? turkey
- Say <u>pil</u>: (pil) Say <u>low</u>: (low) Word? pillow

Now it's your turn. Let's review the instructions:
- I'll say the first syllable and you repeat it.
- Next, I'll say the last syllable and you repeat it.
- Then, tell me the word. Ready?

Say ho: (ho) Say tel: (tel) Word?	hotel	Say mi: (mi) Say nus: (nus) Word?	minus
Say yel: (yel) Say low: (low) Word?	yellow	Say muf: (muf) Say fin: (fin) Word?	muffin
Say ham: (ham) Say ster: (ster) Word?	hamster	Say noi: (noi) Say sy: (sy) Word?	noisy
Say can: (can) Say dle: (dle) Word?	candle	Say ca: (ca) Say ble: (ble) Word?	cable
Say en: (en) Say joy: (joy) Word?	enjoy	Say pen: (pen) Say cil: (cil) Word?	pencil
Say su: (su) Say per: (per) Word?	super	Say let: (let) Say tuce: (tuce) Word?	lettuce
Say num: (num) Say ber: (ber) Word?	number	Say ath: (ath) Say lete: (lete) Word?	athlete
Say ba: (ba) Say gel: (gel) Word?	bagel	Say pho: (pho) Say to: (to) Word?	photo

DAY 3 Letters Ii, Ss, Hh, Bb

Phonological Awareness Warm-Up

PHONOLOGICAL AWARENESS: SYLLABLES

We're going to practice sorting words by their <u>number of syllables</u>. We will use this mat and some pictures to help us. Watch me, my turn.

The word is <u>bus</u>. Bus has 1 syllable. I place bus under the column labeled 1.

Let's practice one together.
- Say <u>pineapple</u>. (pineapple) Let's say it again slowly. (pine-ap-ple)
  - How many syllables are in pineapple? 3
  - Where should we place pineapple? under the column labeled 3

Note: If students need support in counting syllables, use the chin drop or clapping techniques.

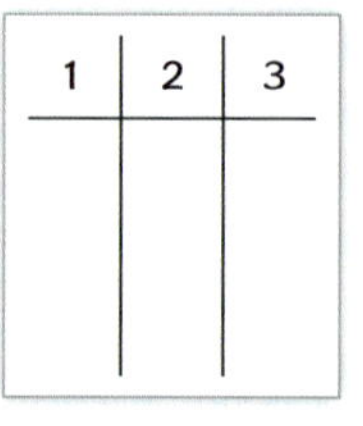

Note:
The pictures used on the Presentation give students a mental image of sorting.

Your turn. Here are the instructions:
- I'll say a word and you repeat it.
- Next, tell me how many syllables the word has and which column it should be placed in. Ready?

Say teacher: (teacher) Syllables? (2) Column?	2	Say unicorn: (unicorn) Syllables? (3) Column?
Say bee: (bee) Syllables? (1) Column?	1	Say house: (house) Syllables? (1) Column?
Say fish: (fish) Syllables? (1) Column?	1	Say mountain: (mountain) Syllables? (2) Column?
Say jelly: (jelly) Syllables? (2) Column?	2	Say soccer: (soccer) Syllables? (2) Column?
Say submarine: (submarine) Syllables? (3) Column?	3	Say camera: (camera) Syllables? (2) Column?
Say waffle: (waffle) Syllables? (2) Column?	2	Say zipper: (zipper) Syllables? (2) Column?
Say ball: (ball) Syllables? (1) Column?	1	Say tree: (tree) Syllables? (1) Column?
Say baby: (baby) Syllables? (2) Column?	2	Say tricycle: (tricycle) Syllables? (3) Column?

Right column values: unicorn 3, house 1, mountain 2, soccer 2, camera 2, zipper 2, tree 1, tricycle 3.

Letter-Sound Correspondence

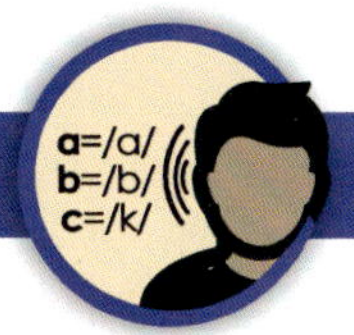

REVIEW OF LETTER-SOUNDS: Ii - /ĭ/, Ss - /s/, Hh - /h/, AND Bb - /b/

Today we will practice the letter names and sounds of 4 letters: Ii, Ss, Hh, and Bb.

There are 2 ways to write each of these letters: uppercase and lowercase.

Let's review these 4 letters. Find letter-sound strip #3.

When I say a letter, place your pointer finger on it and say 3 things: the letter name, the keyword, and the sound.

Let's practice one together. Ready? Place your pointer finger on the uppercase S.
- **Letter name?** uppercase S
- **Keyword?** sun
- **Sound?** /s/

(Mix up your prompts so that you're not asking for the uppercase and lowercase letters next to one another. Ask for each letter at least once.)

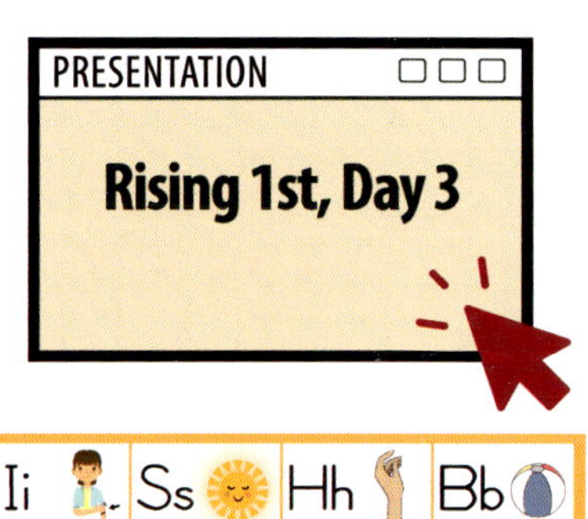

Letter-Sound Correspondence Review				
			Letter Name?	**Keyword?**	**Sound?**
Ii		Uppercase	uppercase I	itch	/ĭ/
		Lowercase	i	itch	/ĭ/
Ss		Uppercase	uppercase S	sun	/s/
		Lowercase	s	sun	/s/
Hh		Uppercase	uppercase H	hand	/h/
		Lowercase	h	hand	/h/
Bb		Uppercase	uppercase B	ball	/b/
		Lowercase	b	ball	/b/

INITIAL SOUND PRACTICE

Now we will look at a picture and write the first sound in the word. Let's do the first one together.

(Display <u>bed</u>.)
Word? bed
- **First sound? /b/**
- **Letter? b**
- **I say /b/ while writing the letter *b*.**

 **Now it's your turn. Turn to page 5 in your Student Workbook.** (Review the name of each picture with students before they begin. Row 1: horse, mop, igloo, seal; Row 2: bat, pin, ghost, itch)

Here are the steps:
1. **Say the word.**
2. **Say the first sound in the word.**
3. **Say the letter.**
4. **Repeat the sound as you write the letter.**

Answer Key

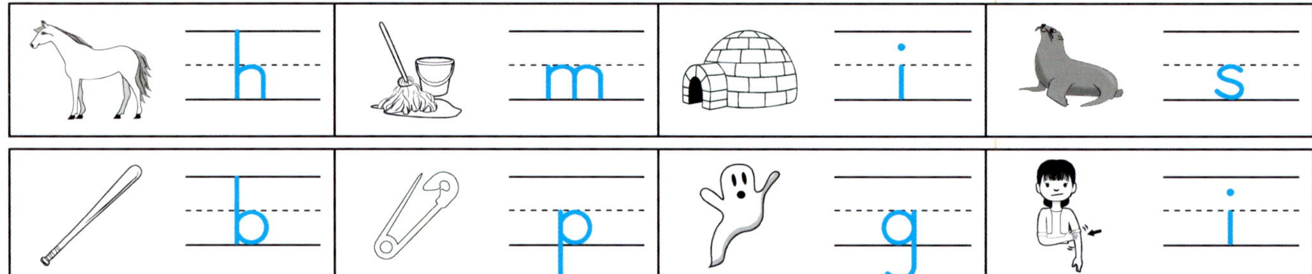

Letter Formation

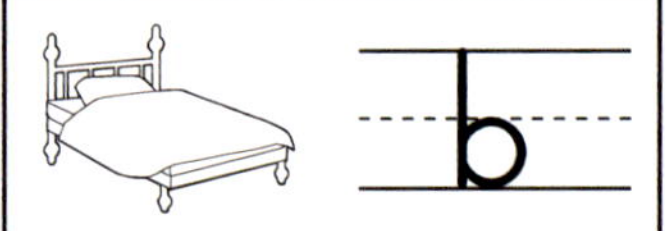

REVIEW LETTER FORMATION: Ii, Ss, Hh, AND Bb

We're going to practice writing the 4 uppercase and lowercase letters we have been studying today.

Watch me write uppercase letter *I*.
1. **Start at the topline, pull down straight. Lift.**
2. **Slide to the right across the top. Lift.**
3. **Slide to the right across the bottom.**

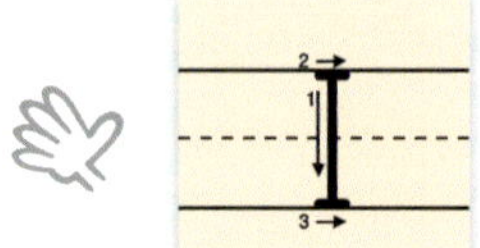

 **Now it's your turn. Turn to page 5 in your Student Workbook. Find the line that has a hand in front of it. We will practice** writing the uppercase letters first.

Letter name? uppercase I Sound? /ĭ/
- Finger ready? Follow the arrows to trace the letter while saying /ĭ/.
- Pencil ready? Follow the arrows to trace the letter while saying /ĭ/.
- Pencil ready? Follow the dotted lines to trace the letter while saying /ĭ/. Do this 2 times.
- Pencil ready? Write the uppercase I until the line is filled. Don't forget to say /ĭ/ as you write it.

(Following the procedure above, repeat the same process with the uppercase letters in this order: S, H, and B. Reference the stroke talk in the table below.)

Stroke Talk for Review of Uppercase Letter Formation – *S, H,* and *B*		
Watch me write uppercase letter _____.		
1. Start just below the topline. Curve back, curve forward, pull along the bottom line, curve up, stop.	1. Pull down straight. Lift. 2. Back to the topline. Pull down straight. Lift. 3. Slide across the midline.	1. Start at the topline. Pull down straight. Lift. 2. Back to the topline. Curve forward. Slide left. 3. Curve forward. Slide left.

Now it's your turn. Find the line that has ___ in front of it.
- Finger ready? Follow the arrow(s) to trace the letter while saying /__/.
- Pencil ready? Follow the arrow(s) to trace the letter while saying /__/.
- Pencil ready? Follow the dotted line(s) to trace the letter while saying /__/. Do this 2 times.
- Pencil ready? Write the uppercase ___ until the line is filled. Don't forget to say /__/ as you write it.

Now let's practice the lowercase letters.
Watch me write the lowercase letter *i*.
1. Start at the midline, pull down straight. Lift.
2. Dot over the top.

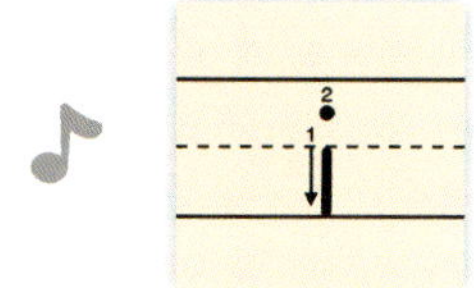

Your turn. Look at the top of page 6 in your workbook. Find the line that has a music note in front of it.

Letter name? i Sound? /ĭ/
- **Finger ready? Follow the arrow to trace the letter while saying /ĭ/.**
- **Pencil ready? Follow the arrow to trace the letter while saying /ĭ/.**
- **Pencil ready? Follow the dotted lines to trace the letter while saying /ĭ/. Do this 2 times.**
- **Pencil ready? Write the lowercase i until the line is filled. Don't forget to say /ĭ/ as you write it.**

(Following the procedure above, repeat the same process with the lowercase letters in this order: s, h, and b. Reference the stroke talk in the table below.)

Stroke Talk for Review of Lowercase Letter Formation – *s*, *h*, and *b*		
Watch me write lowercase letter _____.		
 	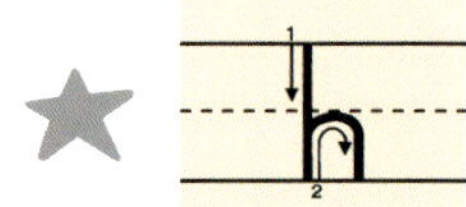	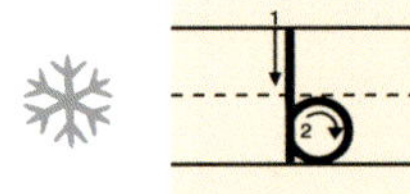
1. Start just below the midline. Curve back, curve forward, pull along the bottom line, curve up, stop.	1. Start at the topline, pull down straight. 2. Push up to the midline, curve forward, pull down straight.	1. Start at the topline. Pull down straight. 2. Push up, circle forward and around.

Now it's your turn. Find the line that has ___ in front of it.
- **Finger ready? Follow the arrow(s) to trace the letter while saying /__/.**
- **Pencil ready? Follow the arrow(s) to trace the letter while saying /__/.**
- **Pencil ready? Follow the dotted line(s) to trace the letter while saying /__/. Do this 2 times.**
- **Pencil ready? Write the lowercase ___ until the line is filled. Don't forget to say /__/ as you write it.**

High-Frequency Words

Now I'm going to show you how to read 4 more high-frequency words. Watch me, my turn.

(Display my.)

The word is my, as in the sentence "My car is red."
- **Watch me finger-stretch the sounds. /m/ /ī/** (Show thumb for /m/ and pointer finger for /ī/.)
- **There are 2 sounds in the word *my*. This word is spelled with 2 letters, *m-y*.**

Now it's your turn. Word? my How many letters? 2
The letter names are m-y. Say them with me. m-y

(Use the process below to review the next 3 words.)

HFW List
is /ĭ/ /z/
like /l/ /ī/ /k/
look /l/ /oo/ /k/

- **The word is _______. What is the word? _______**
- **Listen for this word in the following sentence.** (Use the word in a sentence.)
- **Watch me finger-stretch the sounds.**
- **There are** (number) **sound(s) in the word _______.**
- **This word is spelled with** (number) **letter(s), _______.**

Now it's your turn.
- **Word? _______ How many letter(s)? _______**
- **The letter name(s) are _______. Say them with me. _______**

Note: In the word *is*, the letter *s* is pronounced as /z/. The letter *s* is pronounced /z/ when it follows a voiced consonant or vowel sound (e.g., dogs, words, trees, days, was).

FLUENCY: HIGH-FREQUENCY WORDS

Now we will practice reading the words we have learned.

(Display the high-frequency word grid. Prompt students by saying **"Word?"** at each box.)

like	is	look	my
see	I	you	the
do	a	to	and

Reading

CONCEPTS OF PRINT

When we read, we see letters on a page that make words that can be parts of sentences. Let's review what is different between words and sentences before we practice reading.

The letters we have been reviewing make up the sounds in words. Then, these words can be used to make sentences.

(Point to the sentence on the Presentation file or the first sentence of a book you hold up.)
- **Look at this line.** (Move your finger from left to right.) **This is a sentence.**
- **Notice the first word of this sentence. What is special about the first letter of this word?** (Point to the first word in the sentence on the Presentation file or on a page of the book.) **It is an uppercase letter.**
- **Yes, a sentence always begins with an uppercase letter.**
- (Read a sentence from the Presentation file or from a page of the book. Point to the period.) **Sentences always have a mark after the last word to show us where the sentence ends. This is called a** <u>**period.**</u>

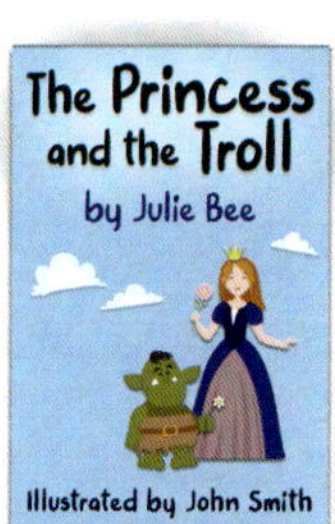

The red dog ran fast into the yard.

READ WORDS & SENTENCES

Today we will read some words and sentences that use the letters we have reviewed the last couple of days.

Turn to page 6 in your workbook and find the line that has a paw print in front of it. We'll read some words and then 3 sentences together.

(Display <u>nap</u>, <u>hit</u>, and <u>had</u>.)

Put your pointer finger in front of the first word and follow along as I read this word.

The word is spelled <u>n-a-p</u>.

- **The first letter is n. The sound of the letter *n* is /n/.**
- **The next letter is a. The sound of the letter *a* is /ă/.**
- **The last letter Is p. The sound of the letter *p* is /p/.**
- **If I say them close together, it is /nnn/.../ăăă/.../p/.**
- **Without pausing, I read the word *nap*, as in the sentence "I need a nap."**

Let's read the next word together. Find the word next to nap that has the letters *h-i-t*.

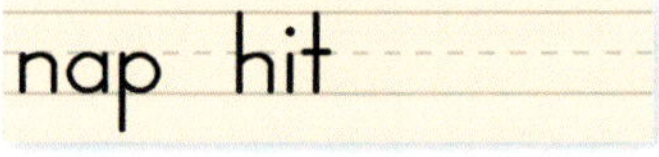

- **Put your finger on the first letter. Say the sound. /h/**
- **Put your finger on the next letter. Say the sound. /ĭ/**
- **Next, put your finger on the last letter. Say the sound. /t/**
- **Sounds? /h/ /ĭ/ /t/** (Point under each letter while saying each sound.)
- **Finally, blend it. Word? hit**

Let's read the next word together. Find the word next to hit that has the letters *h-a-d*.

- **Put your finger on the first letter. Say the sound. /h/**
- **Put your finger on the next letter. Say the sound. /ă/**
- **Next, put your finger on the last letter. Say the sound. /d/**
- **Sounds? /h/ /ă/ /d/** (Point under each letter while saying each sound.)
- **Finally, blend it. Word? had**

I'll give you a minute to practice reading each word 3 more times.

(Display sentences.)

Now we will read sentences. Find the line with the puppy. Put your pointer finger under the first word spelled uppercase N-a-n. Notice how each sentence begins with an uppercase letter. Each of these sentences has 4 words with spaces in between the words, and the sentences end with a period.

Watch me, my turn. (Move your finger from left to right under the sentences as you read.)

Nan had a nap. Now read it with me. Ready?
Nan had a nap.

Listen: Pam hit the bat. Read along with me. Ready?
Pam hit the bat.

Listen: Tim hid the hat. Read along with me. Ready?
Tim hid the hat.

I'll give you a couple minutes to practice whisper reading each sentence again.

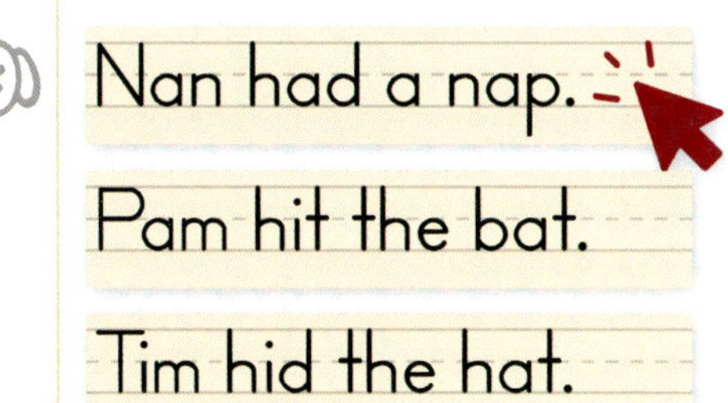

Phonological Awareness Wrap-Up

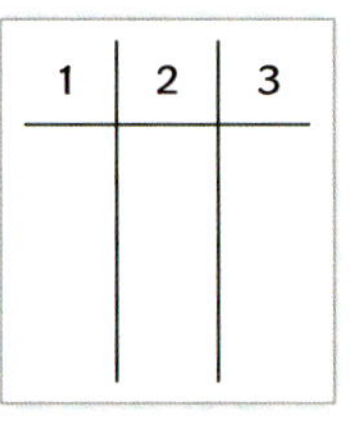

PHONOLOGICAL AWARENESS: SYLLABLES

Let's sort more words based on their number of syllables. Let's review the instructions:
- **I'll say a word and you repeat it.**
- **Next, tell me how many syllables the word has and which column it should be placed in. Ready?**

1	2	3

Say milk: (milk) **Syllables?** (1) **Column?**	1	**Say umbrella:** (umbrella) **Syllables?** (3) **Column?**	3
Say plane: (plane) **Syllables?** (1) **Column?**	1	**Say rug:** (rug) **Syllables?** (1) **Column?**	1
Say butterfly: (butterfly) **Syllables?** (3) **Column?**	3	**Say lightning:** (lightning) **Syllables?** (2) **Column?**	2
Say apple: (apple) **Syllables?** (2) **Column?**	2	**Say towel:** (towel) **Syllables?** (2) **Column?**	2
Say buffalo: (buffalo) **Syllables?** (3) **Column?**	3	**Say dinosaur:** (dinosaur) **Syllables?** (3) **Column?**	3
Say nickel: (nickel) **Syllables?** (2) **Column?**	2	**Say seven:** (seven) **Syllables?** (2) **Column?**	2
Say chair: (chair) **Syllables?** (1) **Column?**	1	**Say sun:** (sun) **Syllables?** (1) **Column?**	1
Say crayon: (crayon) **Syllables?** (2) **Column?**	2	**Say puppy:** (puppy) **Syllables?** (2) **Column?**	2

Day
4

DAY 4 — Letters Oo, Ll, Rr, Cc, Ff, Jj, Ww

Phonological Awareness Warm-Up

PHONOLOGICAL AWARENESS: ONSET-RIME

Today we are going practice <u>changing the onset</u>, or beginning sound, in a word.

We'll keep the ending part the same and change only the beginning sound to make a new word; when we do this, the 2 words rhyme.

Watch me, my turn.
- I say <u>sad</u>. I'll change /s/ to /h/. The new word is <u>had</u>.
- <u>Sad</u> and <u>had</u> rhyme because the last part sounds the same.

Let's do one together.
- Say <u>set</u>: (set) Change /s/ to /g/. Word? get
- Do <u>set</u> and <u>get</u> rhyme? yes

Now it's your turn. Here are the instructions:
- I'll say a word and you repeat it.
- Next, I'll tell you the first sound to change in the word.
- Then, tell me the new word that rhymes. Ready?

Say met: (met) Change /m/ to /l/. Word?	let	Say king: (king) Change /k/ to /r/. Word?	ring
Say bike: (bike) Change /b/ to /h/. Word?	hike	Say day: (day) Change /d/ to /m/. Word?	may
Say lot: (lot) Change /l/ to /n/. Word?	knot	Say white: (white) Change /hw/ to /b/. Word?	bite
Say sash: (sash) Change /s/ to /r/. Word?	rash	Say song: (song) Change /s/ to /l/. Word?	long
Say tile: (tile) Change /t/ to /hw/. Word?	while	Say name: (name) Change /n/ to /g/. Word?	game
Say rug: (rug) Change /r/ to /d/. Word?	dug	Say few: (few) Change /f/ to /d/. Word?	dew
Say lap: (lap) Change /l/ to /k/. Word?	cap	Say rent: (rent) Change /r/ to /t/. Word?	tent
Say jam: (jam) Change /j/ to /p/. Word?	Pam	Say chick: (chick) Change /ch/ to /p/. Word?	pick

Day
4

Letter-Sound Correspondence

REVIEW OF LETTER-SOUNDS: Oo - /ŏ/, Ll - /l/, Rr - /r/, Cc - /k/, Ff - /f/, Jj - /j/, AND Ww - /w/

Today we will practice the letter names and sounds of 7 letters: Oo, Ll, Rr, Cc, Ff, Jj, and Ww.

There are 2 ways to write each of these letters: uppercase and lowercase.

Let's review these 7 letters. Find letter-sound strips #4 and #5.

When I say a letter, place your pointer finger on it and say 3 things: the letter name, the keyword, and the sound.

Let's practice one together. Ready? Place your pointer finger on the uppercase F.

- **Letter name? uppercase F**
- **Keyword? fish**
- **Sound? /f/**

(Mix up your prompts so that you're not asking for the uppercase and lowercase letters next to one another. Ask for each letter at least once.)

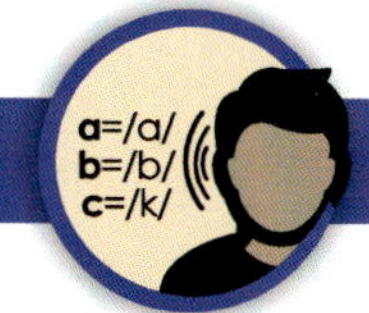

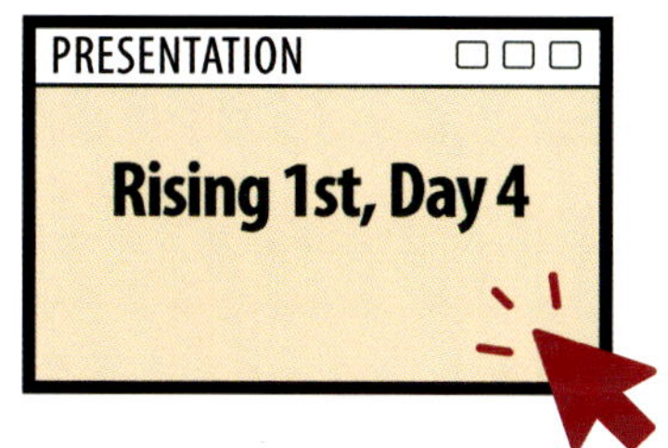

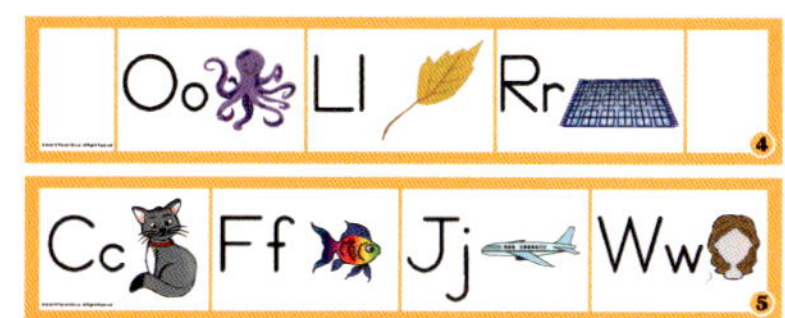

Letter-Sound Correspondence Review				
			Letter Name?	**Keyword?**	**Sound?**
Oo		Uppercase	uppercase O	octopus	/ŏ/
		Lowercase	o	octopus	/ŏ/
Ll		Uppercase	uppercase L	leaf	/l/
		Lowercase	l	leaf	/l/
Rr		Uppercase	uppercase R	rug	/r/
		Lowercase	r	rug	/r/
Cc		Uppercase	uppercase C	cat	/k/
		Lowercase	c	cat	/k/
Ff		Uppercase	uppercase F	fish	/f/
		Lowercase	f	fish	/f/
Jj		Uppercase	uppercase J	jet	/j/
		Lowercase	j	jet	/j/
Ww		Uppercase	uppercase W	wig	/w/
		Lowercase	w	wig	/w/

Day 4

INITIAL SOUND PRACTICE

Now we will look at a picture and write the first sound in the word. Let's do the first one together.

(Display <u>carrot</u>.)
Word? carrot

- **First sound? /k/**
- **Letter name? c**
- **I say /k/ while writing the letter *c*.**

 **Now it's your turn. Turn to page 7 in your Student Workbook.** (Review the name of each picture with students before they begin. Row 1: juggle, fox, watermelon, ostrich; Row 2: lip, rat, cactus, bed)

Here are the steps:

1. **Say the word.**
2. **Say the first sound in the word.**
3. **Say the letter.**
4. **Repeat the sound as you write the letter.**

Answer Key

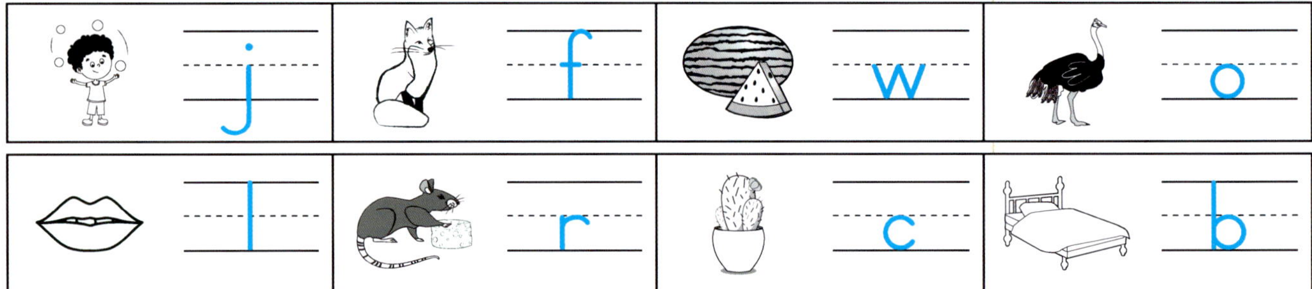

Letter Formation

REVIEW LETTER FORMATION: Oo, LL, Rr, Cc, Ff, Jj, AND Ww

We're going to practice writing the 7 uppercase and lowercase letters we have been studying today.

Watch me write uppercase letter *O*.

1. **Start just below the topline. Circle back and around.**

 **Now it's your turn. Turn to page 7 in your Student Workbook. Find the line that has a shirt in front of it. We will practice writing the uppercase letters first.**

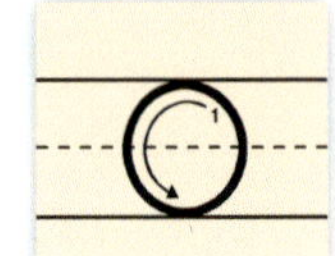

Letter name? uppercase O Sound? /ŏ/

- **Finger ready? Follow the arrow to trace the letter while saying /ŏ/.**
- **Pencil ready? Follow the arrow to trace the letter while saying /ŏ/. Do this 2 times.**
- **Pencil ready? Write the uppercase O 1more time. Don't forget to say /ŏ/ as you write it.**

(Following the procedure above, repeat the same process with the uppercase letters in this order: L, R, C, F, J, and W. Reference the stroke talk in the table below.)

Note: The letter formation of these letters are less complex, so the format in the workbook has changed. There is room for the students to practice each letter 1 time. If students need extra letter formation practice, there are blank writing pages in the back of the Student Workbook.

Stroke Talk for Review of Uppercase Letter Formation – *L, R, C, F, J*, and *W*	
Watch me write uppercase letter ___.	

	1. Start at the topline, pull down straight. 2. Slide right.		1. Pull down straight. Lift. 2. Back to the topline. Slide to the right. Lift. 3. Slide along the midline
	1. Start at the topline. Pull down straight. Lift. 2. Slide along the topline, curve right, slide left. 3. Slant right.		1. Start at the topline, pull down, curve left. Lift. 2. Slide to the right across the top.
	1. Start just below the topline. Circle backward, pull along the bottom line, start up. Stop.		1. Start at the topline. Slant to the right. 2. Slant up. 3. Slant to the right. 4. Slant up.

Now it's your turn. The next letter is uppercase ___.

- **Finger ready? Follow the arrow(s) to trace the letter while saying /_ /.**
- **Pencil ready? Follow the arrow(s) to trace the letter while saying /_ /. Do this 2 times.**
- **Pencil ready? Write the uppercase ___ 1 more time. Don't forget to say /_ / as you write it.**

Now let's practice the lowercase letters.
Watch me write the lowercase letter *o*.

1. **Start just below the midline. Circle back and around.**

 **Your turn. You should still be on page 7 of your workbook. Find the line that has a ghost in front of it.**

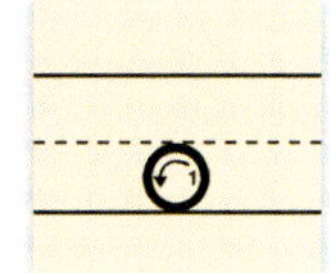

Letter name? o Sound? /ŏ/

- **Finger ready? Follow the arrow to trace the letter while saying /ŏ/.**
- **Pencil ready? Follow the arrow to trace the letter while saying /ŏ/. Do this 2 times.**
- **Pencil ready? Write the lowercase o 1 more time. Don't forget to say /ŏ/ as you write it.**

 95 Phonics Booster Bundle™: Summer School Edition 2021 • Rising First • Teacher's Edition **25**

(Following the procedure on the previous page, repeat the same process with the lowercase letter, in this order: l, r, c, f, j, and w. Reference the stroke talk in the table below.)

Stroke Talk for Review of Lowercase Letter Formation – *l, r, c, f, j,* and *w*	
Watch me write lowercase letter ___.	
1. Start at the topline, pull down straight.	1. Start just below the topline. Curve back, pull down straight. Lift. 2. Slide across the midline.
1. Start at the midline. Pull down straight. 2. Push up, curve right. Stop.	1. Start at the midline, pull down, curve left. Stop. 2. Dot over the top.
1. Start just below the midline. Circle backward, pull along the bottom line, start up. Stop.	1. Start at the midline. Slant to the right. 2. Slant up. 3. Slant to the right. 4. Slant up.

 Now it's your turn. The next letter is ___.

- Finger ready? Follow the arrow(s) to trace the letter while saying /_ /.
- Pencil ready? Follow the arrow(s) to trace the letter while saying /_ /. Do this 2 times.
- Pencil ready? Write the lowercase ___ 1 more time. Don't forget to say /_ / as you write it.

High-Frequency Words

Now I'm going to show you how to read 4 more high-frequency words. Watch me, my turn.

(Display <u>for</u>.)

The word is <u>for</u>, as in the sentence "It is for my mom."

- **Watch me finger-stretch the sounds. /f/ /or/** (Show thumb for /f/ and pointer finger for /or/.)
- **There are 2 sounds in the word *for*. This word is spelled with 3 letters, *f-o-r*.**

Now it's your turn. Word? for How many letters? 3
The letter names are f-o-r. Say them with me. f-o-r

(Use the process on the next page to review the next 3 words.)

HFW List
said /s/ /ĕ/ /d/
want /w/ /ŭ/ /n/ /t/
who /h/ /ū/

- **The word is _______. What is the word? _______**
- **Listen for this word in the following sentence.** (Use the word in a sentence.)
- **Watch me finger-stretch the sounds.**
- **There are** (number) **sound(s) in the word _______.**
- **This word is spelled with** (number) **letter(s), _______. ·**

Now it's your turn.
- **Word? _______ How many letter(s)? _______**
- **The letter name(s) are _______. Say them with me. _______**

FLUENCY: HIGH-FREQUENCY WORDS

Now we will practice reading the words we know.

(Display the high-frequency word grid. Prompt students by saying **"Word?"** at each box.)

want	for	who	said
is	see	and	my
do	a	like	to
I	look	you	the

Note: Starting with this lesson, the fluency table for high-frequency words has increased from 12 words to 16 words.

Reading

READ SENTENCES

It's sentence time!

Turn to page 8 in your workbook. Find the line that has a hanger in front of it.

(Display word box.)
Above the line, there is a box with some high-frequency words in it. Let's read them together. is, my, I, like, to, said, look, do, you, see

is, my, I, like, to, said, look, do, you, see

(Display sentence.)
Now, put your pointer finger in front of the first word in the first sentence. Let's read this first sentence together. When you see a bold word—"bold" means it is darker than the other words—it is a high-frequency word. We will read these words instead of sounding them out.

- **How many words do you see?** 5
- **How is the first word spelled?** uppercase M-a-c **This word is not bold, so we will will say the sounds before reading the word.**
  - **First sound?** /m/ **Second sound?** /ă/ **Last sound?** /k/ **Word?** Mac
  - **Notice that M is an uppercase letter because it begins the first word in the sentence, and it is also a name.**

- How is the second word spelled? **i-s**
  - The letters *i-s* spell the bold high-frequency word *is*.
  - What word? **is**
- How is the third word spelled? **m-y**
  - The letters *m-y* spell the bold high-frequency word *my*.
  - What word? **my**
- How is the fourth word spelled? **b-i-g** Is it bold? **no** Let's say the sounds.
  - First sound? **/b/** Next sound? **/ĭ/** Last sound? **/g/** Word? **big**
- How is the last word spelled? **p-i-g** Is it bold? **no** Let's say the sounds.
  - First sound? **/p/** Next sound? **/ĭ/** Last sound? **/g/** Word? **pig**
- Which punctuation mark is at the end? **a period**
- Now read the sentence. **Mac is my big pig.**

Now it is your turn to read. **On page 8, you will see there are 3 more sentences after the sentence we just read together.**

Let's review the steps:
1. Put your finger under each word.
   - If the word is bold, it's a high-frequency word. Read the word.
   - If it's not a high-frequency word, point to the letters, say the sounds, and then read the word.
2. Continue until you read each word.
3. Then read the sentence.

(After reading the sentences, ask the students what the kid likes to do with the pig. **The kid likes to sit on the pig.**)

> 1. **I like to** sit on **my** pig.
> 2. Mom **said to look** at Mac.
> 3. **Do you see** him?

Note: To encourage language development, remind the students to orally answer the question in a complete sentence.

Phonological Awareness Wrap-Up

PHONOLOGICAL AWARENESS: ONSET-RIME

Now, we are going to practice <u>changing the onset</u>, or beginning sound, in a word. Let's review the instructions:
- I'll say a word and you repeat it.
- Next, I'll tell you the first sound to change in the word.
- Then, tell me the new word that rhymes. Ready?

Say toy: (toy) Change /t/ to /r/. Word?	**Roy**	Say whale: (whale) Change /hw/ to /m/. Word?	**male**
Say sob: (sob) Change /s/ to /n/. Word?	**knob**	Say lack: (lack) Change /l/ to /r/. Word?	**rack**
Say pile: (pile) Change /p/ to /hw/. Word?	**while**	Say hen: (hen) Change /h/ to /p/. Word?	**pen**
Say call: (call) Change /k/ to /b/. Word?	**ball**	Say bug: (bug) Change /b/ to /r/. Word?	**rug**
Say wade: (wade) Change /w/ to /sh/. Word?	**shade**	Say chime: (chime) Change /ch/ to /t/. Word?	**time**
Say late: (late) Change /l/ to /k/. Word?	**Kate**	Say seal: (seal) Change /s/ to /r/. Word?	**real**
Say near: (near) Change /n/ to /f/. Word?	**fear**	Say mad: (mad) Change /m/ to /s/. Word?	**sad**
Say tight: (tight) Change /t/ to /s/. Word?	**sight**	Say rake: (rake) Change /r/ to /l/. Word?	**lake**

DAY 5   Letters Ee, Zz, Kk, Yy, Vv, Uu, Qq, Xx

Phonological Awareness Warm-Up

PHONOLOGICAL AWARENESS: PHONEME ISOLATION – FIRST & LAST SOUND

Today we are going to practice saying the <u>first or last sound</u> in a word.

Watch me, my turn.
- I say <u>take</u>. The beginning sound is /t/.

Let's practice one together.
- Say <u>fight</u>. (fight) Beginning sound? /f/

Now watch me say the last sound in a word.
- I say <u>fan</u>. The last sound is /n/.

Let's practice one together.
- Say <u>trash</u>. (trash) Last sound? /sh/

Now it's your turn. Here are the instructions:
- I'll say a word and you repeat it.
- Then, I'll ask you to tell me the first or last sound. Ready?

Say add: (add) First sound?	/ă/	Say dug: (dug) Last sound?	/g/
Say honk: (honk) First sound?	/h/	Say toe: (toe) Last sound?	/ō/
Say bush: (bush) First sound?	/b/	Say lane: (lane) Last sound?	/n/
Say yet: (yet) First sound?	/y/	Say much: (much) Last sound?	/ch/
Say joke: (joke) First sound?	/j/	Say match: (match) Last sound?	/ch/
Say save: (save) First sound?	/s/	Say pin: (pin) Last sound?	/n/
Say net: (net) First sound?	/n/	Say fish: (fish) Last sound?	/sh/
Say boo: (boo) First sound?	/b/	Say pink: (pink) Last sound?	/k/

Letter-Sound Correspondence

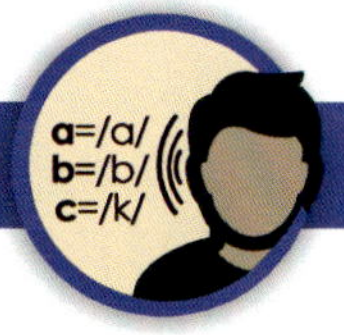

REVIEW OF LETTER-SOUNDS: Ee - /ĕ/, Zz - /z/, Kk - /k/, Yy - /y/, Vv - /v/, Uu - /ŭ/, Qq - /k/ /w/, AND Xx - /k/ /s/

Today we will practice the letter names and sounds of 8 letters: Ee, Zz, Kk, Yy, Vv, Uu, Qq, and Xx.

There are 2 ways to write each of these letters: uppercase and lowercase.
- What are examples of when we would write or see an uppercase letter? the first word in a sentence, the first letter in a name, a special place

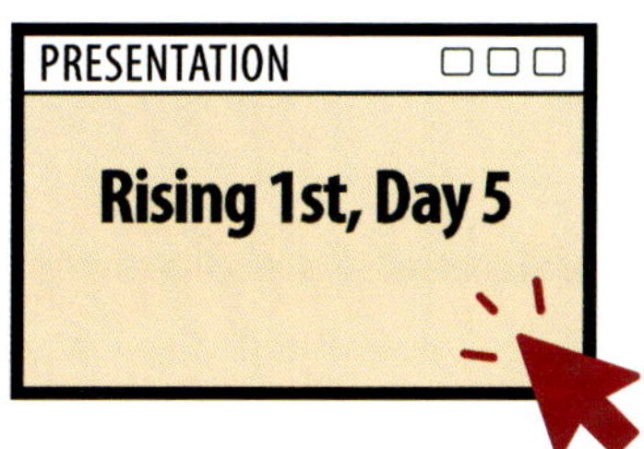

Let's review these 8 letters. Find letter-sound strips #6 and #7. When I say a letter, place your pointer finger on it and say 3 things: the letter name, the keyword, and the sound.

Let's practice one together. Ready? Place your pointer finger on the uppercase E.
- **Letter name?** uppercase E
- **Keyword?** echo
- **Sound?** /ĕ/

(Mix up your prompts so that you're not asking for the uppercase and lowercase letters next to one another. Ask for each letter at least once.)

Letter-Sound Correspondence Review			Letter Name?	Keyword?	Sound?
Ee		Uppercase	uppercase E	echo	/ĕ /
		Lowercase	e	echo	/ĕ/
Zz		Uppercase	uppercase Z	zipper	/z/
		Lowercase	z	zipper	/z/
Kk		Uppercase	uppercase K	kite	/k/
		Lowercase	k	kite	/k/
Yy		Uppercase	uppercase Y	yo-yo	/y/
		Lowercase	y	yo-yo	/y/
Vv		Uppercase	uppercase V	van	/v/
		Lowercase	v	van	/v/
Uu		Uppercase	uppercase U	up	/ŭ/
		Lowercase	u	up	/ŭ/
Qq		Uppercase	uppercase Q	queen	/k/ /w/
		Lowercase	q	queen	/k/ /w/
Xx		Uppercase	uppercase X	box	/k/ /s/
		Lowercase	x	box	/k/ /s/

Note: The letters *q* and *x* are comprised of 2 sounds. For example, the word *box* has 4 sounds, /b/ /ŏ/ /k/ /s/. The word *queen* has 4 sounds, /k/ /w/ /ē/ /n/.

INITIAL SOUND PRACTICE

Now we will look at a picture and write the first or last sound in the word. Let's start by reviewing 1 of the sounds we've learned. The letter *x* is most often found at the ends of words.

(Display box.)
Word? box
- **Last sounds?** /k/ /s/
- **Letter?** x
- **I say /k/ /s/ while writing the letter *x*.**

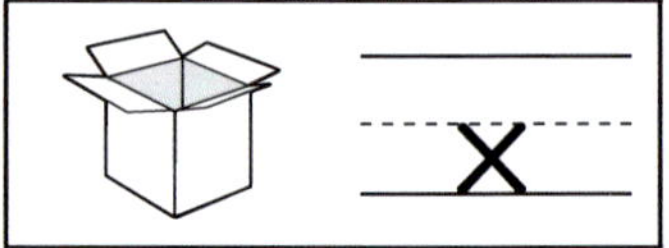

Now it's your turn. Turn to page 8 in your Student Workbook.
(Review the name of each picture with students before they begin.
Row 1: fox, quilt, zoo, umbrella; Row 2: vest, king, enter, yarn)

Here are the steps:
1. **Say the word.**
2. **Say the first sound in the word, except for fox where you'll say and write the last sound.**
3. **Say the letter.**
4. **Repeat the sound as you write the letter.**

Answer Key

x	q	z	u
v	k	e	y

Letter Formation

REVIEW LETTER FORMATION: Ee, Zz, Kk, Yy, Vv, Uu, Qq, & Xx

We're going to practice writing the 8 uppercase and lowercase letters we have been studying today.

Watch me write uppercase letter *E*.
1. **Pull down straight. Lift.**
2. **Back to the topline. Slide to the right. Lift.**
3. **Slide along the midline. Lift.**
4. **Slide along the bottom line.**

Now it's your turn. Turn to page 8 in your Student Workbook. Find the line that has a snowman in front of it. We will practice writing the uppercase letters first.

Letter name? uppercase E **Sound?** /ĕ/
- **Finger ready? Follow the arrows to trace the letter while saying /ĕ/.**
- **Pencil ready? Follow the arrows to trace the letter while saying /ĕ/. Do this 2 times.**
- **Pencil ready? Write the uppercase E 1 more time. Don't forget to say /ĕ/ as you write it.**

(Following the procedure on the previous page, repeat the same process with the uppercase letters in this order: Z, K, Y, V, U, Q, and X . Reference the stroke talk in the table below.)

Stroke Talk for Review of Uppercase Letter Formation – *Z, K, Y, V, U, Q,* and *X*	
Watch me write uppercase letter ____.	
1. Start at the topline. Slide right. 2. Slant left. 3. Slide right.	1. Start at the topline. Pull down, curve around, push up to the topline.
1. Start at the topline, pull down straight. Lift. 2. Start at the topline, slant left to the midline. 3. Slant right.	1. Start just below the topline. Circle back and around. Lift. 2. Short slant right.
1. Start at the topline. Slant right to the midline. Lift. 2. Start at the topline. Slant left to the midline. Pull down straight.	1. Start at the topline. Slant right. Lift. 2. Back to the topline. Slant left.
1. Start at the topline. Slant to the right. 2. Slant up.	

 Now it's your turn. The next letter is uppercase ___.

- Finger ready? Follow the arrow(s) to trace the letter while saying /__/.
- Pencil ready? Follow the arrow(s) to trace the letter while saying /__/. Do this 2 times.
- Pencil ready? Write the uppercase ___ 1 more time. Don't forget to say /__/ as you write it.

Now let's practice the lowercase letters.

Watch me write the <u>lowercase letter *e*</u>.

1. **Start in the middle. Slide to the right.**
2. **Curve back. Pull along the bottom line, start up. Stop.**

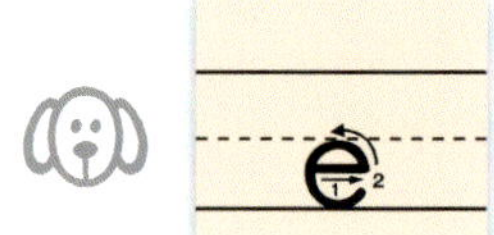

Your turn. Look at the top of page 9 in your workbook. Find the line that has a puppy in front of it.

Letter name? e Sound? /ĕ/

- **Finger ready? Follow the arrows to trace the letter while saying /ĕ/.**
- **Pencil ready? Follow the arrows to trace the letter while saying /ĕ/. Do this 2 times.**
- **Pencil ready? Write the lowercase e 1 more time. Don't forget to say /ĕ/ as you write it.**

(Following the procedure on the previous page, repeat the same process with the lowercase letters in this order: z, k, y, v, u, q, and x. Reference the stroke talk in the table below.)

Stroke Talk for Review of Lowercase Letter Formation – *z, k, y, v, u, q,* and *x*	
Watch me write lowercase letter _____.	
1. Start at the midline. Slide right. 2. Slant left. 3. Slide right.	1. Start at the midline. Pull down, curve around, push up. 2. Pull down straight.
1. Start at the topline, pull down straight. Lift. 2. Slant left from the midline. 3. Slant right.	1. Start just below the midline. Circle back and around, push up. 2. Pull down straight, curve right. Stop.
1. Start at the midline. Slant right. Lift. 2. Slant left down low.	1. Start at the midline. Slant right. Lift. 2. Back to the midline. Slant left.
1. Start at the midline. Slant to the right. 2. Slant up.	

 **Now it's your turn. The next letter is ___.**

- Finger ready? Follow the arrows to trace the letter while saying /__/.
- Pencil ready? Follow the arrows to trace the letter while saying /__/. Do this 2 times.
- Pencil ready? Write the lowercase ___ 1 more time. Don't forget to say /__/ as you write it.

High-Frequency Words

Now I'm going to show you how to read 4 more high-frequency words. Watch me, my turn.

(Display now.)
The word is now, as in the sentence "We will go now."
- **Watch me finger-stretch the sounds. /n/ /ou/** (Show thumb for /n/ and pointer finger for /ou/.)
- **There are 2 sounds in the word *now*. This word is spelled with 3 letters, *n-o-w*.**

Now it's your turn. Word? now How many letters? 3
The letter names are n-o-w. Say them with me. n-o-w

(Use the process below to review the next 3 words.)

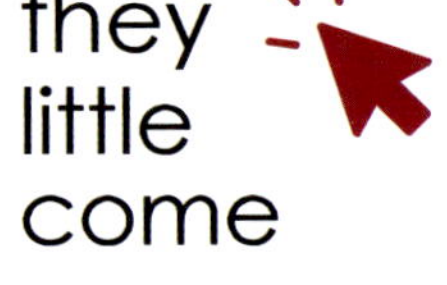

HFW List
they /<u>th</u>/ /ā/
little /l/ /ĭ/ /t/ /əl/
come /k/ /ŭ/ /m/

- **The word is ______. What is the word?** ______
- **Listen for this word in the following sentence.** (Use the word in a sentence.)
- **Watch me finger-stretch the sounds.**
- **There are** (number) **sound(s) in the word** ______.
- **This word is spelled with** (number) **letter(s),** ______.

Now it's your turn.
- **Word?** ______ **How many letter(s)?** ______
- **The letter name(s) are** ______. **Say them with me.** ______

Note: Consonant-le spellings, as in the word *little*, often occur in unstressed syllables, creating a reduced vowel sound (or a schwa sound) that moves quickly into the /l/ sound.

FLUENCY: HIGH-FREQUENCY WORDS

Now we will practice reading the words we know.

(Display the high-frequency word grid. Prompt students by saying **"Word?"** at each box.)

they	now	come	little
who	like	see	look
want	and	do	said
my	you	the	for

Reading

READ SENTENCES

It's sentence time!

 **Turn to page 9 in your workbook. Find the line that has a star in front of it.**

(Display word box.)
Above the line, there is a box with some high-frequency words that we have learned. Let's read them together. they, the, is, little, do, you, want, to, come

they, the, is, little, do,
you, want, to, come

(Display sentence.)
Now, put your pointer finger in front of the first word in the sentence. Let's read the first sentence together. Remember, if the word is bold, it is a high-frequency word. We will read the word without sounding it out.

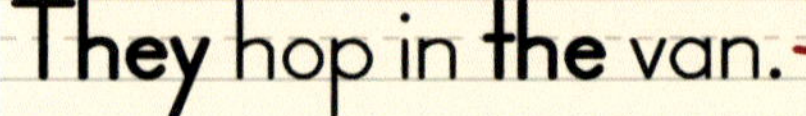

- **How many words do you see?** 5
- **How is the first word spelled?** uppercase T-h-e-y
    - **The letters** *t-h-e-y* **spell the bold high-frequency word** *they*.
    - **What word?** they
    - **Notice that T is an uppercase letter because it begins the first word in the sentence.**

- How is the second word spelled? **h-o-p** This word is not bold. Let's say the sounds.
  - First sound? **/h/** Second sound? **/ŏ/** Last sound? **/p/** Word? **hop**
- How is the third word spelled? **i-n** This word is not bold. Let's say the sounds.
  - First sound? **/ĭ/** Last sound? **/n/** Word? **in**
- How is the fourth word spelled? **t-h-e**
  - The letters *t-h-e* spell the bold high-frequency word *the*.
  - What word? **the**
- How is the last word spelled? **v-a-n** This word is not bold. Let's say the sounds.
  - First sound? **/v/** Next sound? **/ă/** Last sound? **/n/** Word? **van**
- Which punctuation mark is at the end? **a period**
- Now read the sentence. **They hop in the van.**

Now it is your turn to read. On page 9, you will see there are 3 more sentences after the sentence we just read together.

Let's review the steps:
1. Put your finger under each word.
   - If the word is bold, it's a high-frequency word. Read the word.
   - If it's not a high-frequency word, point to the letters, say the sounds, and then read the word.
2. Continue until you read each word.
3. Then read the sentence.

(After reading, discuss how the sentences tell a story. Ask the students what size the van is. **The van is little.**)

1. **The** van **is little**.
2. **Do you want to come**?
3. **The little** van **is** fun.

Phonological Awareness Wrap-Up

PHONOLOGICAL AWARENESS: PHONEME ISOLATION—FIRST & LAST SOUND

Now we are going to practice saying the first or last sound in a word. Listen carefully because sometimes I will ask you to say the first sound, and other times I will ask you to say the last sound. Let's review the instructions:

- I'll say a word and you'll repeat it.
- Then, I'll ask you to tell me the first or last sound. Ready?

Say dash: (**dash**) First sound?	**/d/**	Say ten: (**ten**) Last sound?	**/n/**
Say won: (**won**) First sound?	**/w/**	Say ship: (**ship**) Last sound?	**/p/**
Say robe: (**robe**) Last sound?	**/b/**	Say some: (**some**) First sound?	**/s/**
Say right: (**right**) Last sound?	**/t/**	Say June: (**June**) First sound?	**/j/**
Say rice: (**rice**) Last sound?	**/s/**	Say aid: (**aid**) First sound?	**/ā/**
Say rip: (**rip**) First sound?	**/r/**	Say bun: (**bun**) Last sound?	**/n/**
Say put: (**put**) First sound?	**/p/**	Say fudge: (**fudge**) Last sound?	**/j/**
Say eat: (**eat**) First sound?	**/ē/**	Say soon: (**soon**) Last sound?	**/n/**

Day 6

Days 6–10: Short Vowels, Reading, & Writing 1

Learning Objective

Students demonstrate understanding of how to read sentences and short stories with decodable VC and CVC words and selected irregularly spelled high-frequency words. Additionally, they write short sentences composed of these types of words.

DAY 6

Phonological Awareness Warm-Up

PHONOLOGICAL AWARENESS: BLENDING 2-PHONEME WORDS

Today we are going to practice <u>blending 2 sounds</u> to say a word.

Watch me, my turn.
- I say 2 sounds. /m/ /ā/
- Next, I blend the sounds to say a word. <u>may</u>

Let's practice together. I'll answer with you.
- Listen to the sounds. /b/ /ī/: Word? **bye**
- /m/ /ē/: Word? **me**

Now it's your turn. Let's review the instructions:
- I'll say the sounds.
- Then, I'll ask you to tell me the word. Ready?

/h/ /ā/: Word?	**hay**	/ē/ /ch/: Word?	**each**
/m/ /ō/: Word?	**mow**	/s/ /ī/: Word?	**sigh**
/s/ /ō/: Word?	**sew**	/ă/ /m/: Word?	**am**
/t/ /ū/: Word?	**to**	/k/ /ou/: Word?	**cow**
/ĭ/ /t/: Word?	**it**	/p/ /ī/: Word?	**pie**
/ă/ /z/: Word?	**as**	/m/ /ā/: Word?	**may**
/m/ /ū/: Word?	**moo**	/n/ /ē/: Word?	**knee**
/r/ /ō/: Word?	**row**	/sh/ /ū/: Word?	**shoe**

Letter-Sound Correspondence

WORD COMPLETION WITH PICTURES

Now we're going to fill in the missing sounds in words. Look at each picture. Fill in the correct letter to complete the word. After you write the letter, whisper read the word.

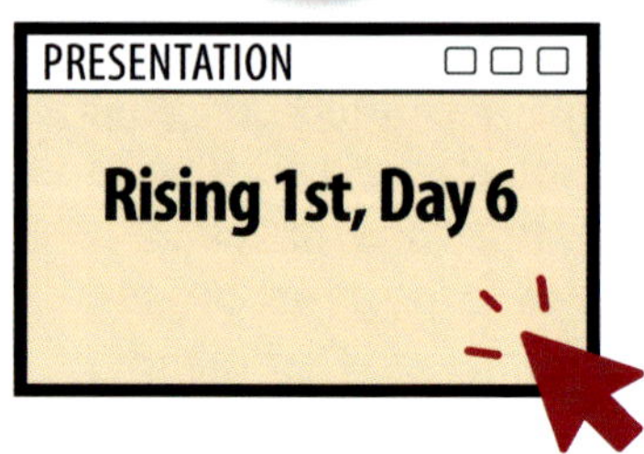

(Display <u>bed</u>.)
I'll do the first one. This picture is <u>bed</u>.
- **I finger-stretch bed. /b/ /ĕ/ /d/**
- **I tap the letters and line while saying the sounds to see what sound is missing.** (Tap the line, the letter *e*, and the letter *d*.)
  - **The first sound /b/ is missing. The sound /b/ is spelled with the letter *b*.**
- **Next, I write the letter *b* in the space.**
- **Finally, I slide a finger under the word and whisper "bed."**

 **Now it's your turn. Turn to page 12 in your Student Workbook.** (Review the name of each picture with students before they begin.)

Here are the steps:
1. **Finger-stretch the sounds.**
2. **Tap the letters and line while saying the sounds.**
3. **Write the letter for the missing sound.**
4. **Whisper read the word.**

Answer Key

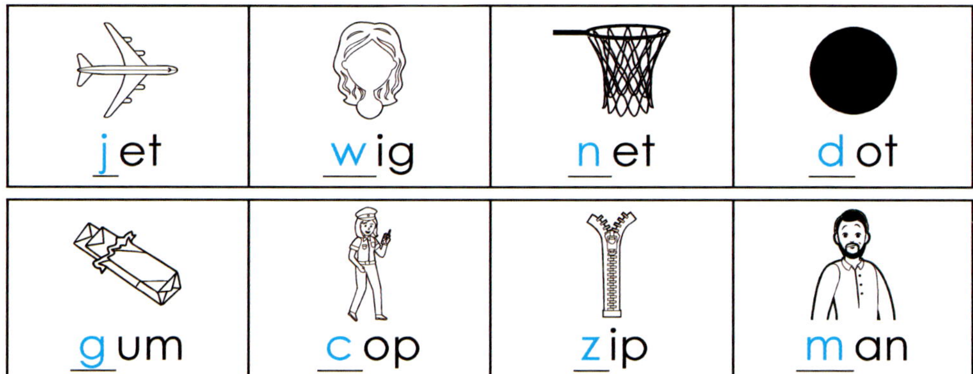

High-Frequency Words

Now I'm going to show you how to read 4 more high-frequency words. Watch me, my turn.

(Display <u>down</u>.)
The word is <u>down</u>, as in the sentence "I went down the hill."
- **Watch me finger-stretch the sounds. /d/ /ou/ /n/** (Show thumb for /d/, pointer finger for /ou/, and middle finger for /n/.)
- **There are 3 sounds in the word *down*. This word is spelled with 4 letters, *d-o-w-n*.**

Now it's your turn. Word? down How many letters? 4
The letter names are d-o-w-n. Say them with me. d-o-w-n

Day
6

(Use the process below to review the next 3 words.)

HFW List
has /h/ /ă/ /z/
have /h/ /ă/ /v/
what /hw/ /ŭ/ /t/

- **The word is _______. What is the word? _______**
- **Listen for this word in the following sentence.** (Use the word in a sentence.)
- **Watch me finger-stretch the sounds.**
- **There are** <u>(number)</u> **sound(s) in the word _______.**
- **This word is spelled with** <u>(number)</u> **letter(s), _______.**

Now it's your turn.
- **Word? _______ How many letter(s)? _______**
- **The letter name(s) are _______. Say them with me. _______**

Note: The sound for the digraph *wh* in the word *what* is called a glide. It is called a glide because the sound glides immediately into the vowel. The sound is created as though it were /hw/, with a slight puff of air before the /w/.

FLUENCY: HIGH-FREQUENCY WORDS

Now we will practice reading the words we know.

(Display the high-frequency word grid. Prompt students by saying **"Word?"** at each box.)

have	down	what	has
they	come	said	who
now	little	for	want
you	do	and	like

Reading

READ SENTENCES

It's sentence time!

 **Turn to page 13 in your workbook. Find the line that has a star in front of it.**

(Display the word boxes.)
Above the line, there are 2 boxes with some high-frequency words that we have learned. The long box at the top of the page has 16 of the 20 high-frequency words we learned in Days 1–5. This box appears on the top of most pages in your workbook starting with today's lesson. The 16-word box is there to help you when you are reading and writing. Point to each word in the 16-word box as we read them together. (Read the 16 words aloud with the students.)

a	and	come	do	for	is	like	look	said	see	the	they	to	want	who	you

Now look at the smaller box below the 16-word box. These are newer high-frequency words or words not included in the longer box. Let's read them together. **down, what, has** Now, put your pointer finger in front of the first word in the sentence. Remember, if the word is bold, it is a high-frequency word. We read the word without sounding it out.

down, what, has

(Display sentence.)
Answer with me as we read the first sentence together.

Kip **said,** "**Look down.**"

- How many words do you see? **4**
- How is the first word spelled? **uppercase K-i-p**
  - First sound? **/k/** Next sound? **/ĭ/** Last sound? **/p/** Word? **Kip**
  - Notice that K is an uppercase letter because it is the first word in the sentence and the first letter of a name.
- How is the second word spelled? **s-a-i-d** This is the bold high-frequency word *said*.
- How is the third word spelled? **uppercase L-o-o-k** This is the bold high-frequency word *look*.
- How is the fourth word spelled? **d-o-w-n** This is the bold high-frequency word *down*.
- What punctuation mark is after the word *down*? **a period**
- Now read the sentence. **Kip said, "Look down."**

Notice the marks before the word *Look* and after the period at the end of the sentence. These marks are called quotation marks. Repeat it with me. **quotation marks**

Quotation marks show us when someone is talking. In this sentence, the quotation marks tell us that Kip is talking and he said, "Look down." We will see quotation marks in the story we will read this week. Keep an eye out for them.

Now it's your turn. On the line that has a star in front of it, find the sentence that is next to the one we just read together. Put your pointer finger in front of the first word.

Let's review the steps:
1. Put your finger under each word.
   - If the word is bold, it's a high-frequency word. Read the word.
   - If it's not a high-frequency word, point to the letters, say the sounds, and then read the word.
2. Continue until you read each word.
3. Then read the sentence.

1. **What is** it?
2. It **is a** bug.
3. It **has a** red dot.

(After reading, discuss how the sentences tell a story. Ask students what Kip saw. **Kip saw a bug.**)

Day
6

Writing

WRITE SENTENCES

Now we'll practice writing sentences. The first word in a sentence starts with an uppercase letter, and there's a punctuation mark at the end like a period or question mark.

Answer with me as we do the first one together.

Let's write the following sentence: <u>I have a pup.</u> Repeat it with me.
I have a pup. (Hold up 1 finger for each word as you repeat the sentence.)
- How many words do you hear? 4
- What is the first word? I I write the high-frequency word spelled uppercase I.
- (Repeat the sentence.) **What is the second word? have** I write the high-frequency word spelled h-a-v-e.
- (Repeat the sentence.) **What is the third word? a** I write the high-frequency word spelled a.
- (Repeat the sentence.) **What is the next word? pup**
  - Sounds and letters? /p/ p - /ŭ/ u - /p/ p
- **Punctuation mark? period**
- **Read the sentence. I have a pup.**

 Now it's your turn. Turn to page 13 in your Student Workbook. Find the line that has a house in front of it.

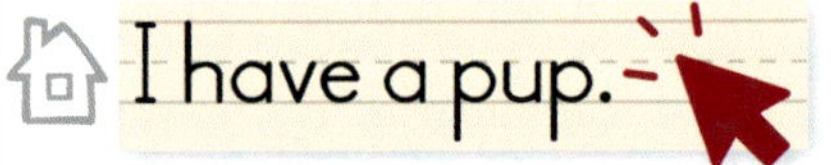

(Display word box.)
Above the line, there is a box that has some high-frequency words that we have learned. Let's read them together. was, I, down

was, I, down

Here are the steps:
1. I'll say the sentence and you repeat it.
2. I'll say each word, and before you write it, decide if it's a high-frequency word. Use the word boxes in your workbook to help you.
   - If it's a high-frequency word, write the letters.
   - If it's not a high-frequency word, break the word into sounds and write the letter for each sound.
3. Make sure the first letter in your sentence is uppercase.
4. Put a punctuation mark at the end.
5. Then, read the sentence.

1. The pup was mad.
2. I set him down.
3. See him run.

Now that you have written 3 sentences, go back to the top and trace the first sentence. Finally, whisper read all 4 sentences.

Phonological Awareness Wrap-Up

PHONOLOGICAL AWARENESS: BLENDING 2-PHONEME WORDS

Today we are going to practice <u>blending 2 sounds</u> to say a word.

Let's practice together. I'll answer with you.
- **Listen to the sounds. /s/ /ā/: Word?** say
- **/sh/ /ē/: Word?** she

Now it's your turn. Let's review the instructions:
- I'll say the sounds.
- Then, I'll ask you to tell me the word. Ready?

/ā/ /p/: Word?	ape	/w/ /ē/: Word?	we
/t/ /ō/: Word?	toe	/ĕ/ /j/: Word?	edge
/h/ /ī/: Word?	high	/ou/ /ch/: Word?	ouch
/ĭ/ /f/: Word?	if	/ē/ /t/: Word?	eat
/b/ /ō/: Word?	bow	/ĕ/ /d/: Word?	Ed
/ŭ/ /s/: Word?	us	/ĭ/ /z/: Word?	is
/ā/ /t/: Word?	ate	/ă/ /t/: Word?	at
/ō/ /k/: Word?	oak	/j/ /ō/: Word?	Joe

DAY 7

Phonological Awareness Warm-Up

PHONOLOGICAL AWARENESS: BLENDING 2-PHONEME WORDS

Today we are going to practice <u>blending 2 sounds</u> to say a word.

Let's practice together. I'll answer with you.
- **Listen to the sounds. /h/ /ē/: Word?** he
- **/ŭ/ /p/: Word?** up

Now it's your turn. Let's review the instructions:
- I'll say the sounds.
- Then, I'll ask you to tell me the word. Ready?

/n/ /ō/: Word?	no	/ĭ/ /ch/: Word?	itch
/s/ /ē/: Word?	see	/t/ /ī/: Word?	tie
/ă/ /sh/: Word?	ash	/g/ /ī/: Word?	guy
/ŏ/ /n/: Word?	on	/k/ /ē/: Word?	key
/h/ /ō/: Word?	hoe	/m/ /ī/: Word?	my
/y/ /ā/: Word?	yay	/sh/ /ī/: Word?	shy
/b/ /oi/: Word?	boy	/ō/ /n/: Word?	own
/b/ /ē/: Word?	bee	/d/ /ō/: Word?	doe

High-Frequency Words

Now I'm going to show you how to read 4 more high-frequency words. Watch me, my turn.

(Display are.)

The word is are, as in the sentence "Where are you going?"
- **Watch me finger-stretch the sounds. /ar/** (Show thumb for /ar/.)
- **There is 1 sound in the word *are*. This word is spelled with 3 letters, *a-r-e*.**

Now it's your turn. Word? are How many letters? 3
The letter names are a-r-e. Say them with me. a-r-e

(Use the process below to review the next 3 words.)

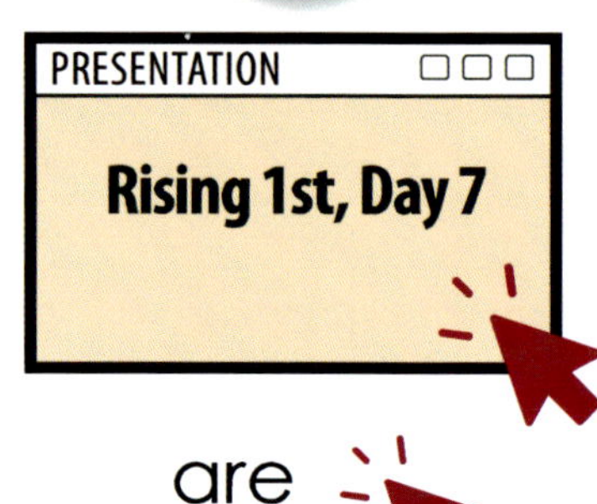

HFW List
good /g/ /oo/ /d/
jump /j/ /ŭ/ /m/ /p/
this /th/ /ĭ/ /s/

- **The word is ______. What is the word? ______**
- **Listen for this word in the following sentence.** (Use the word in a sentence.)
- **Watch me finger-stretch the sounds.**
- **There are (number) sound(s) in the word ______.**
- **This word is spelled with (number) letter(s), ______.**

Now it's your turn.
- **Word? ______ How many letter(s)? ______**
- **The letter name(s) are ______. Say them with me. ______**

FLUENCY: HIGH-FREQUENCY WORDS

Now we will practice reading the words we know.

(Display the high-frequency word grid. Prompt students by saying **"Word?"** at each box.)

jump	are	this	good
has	down	they	now
said	for	what	come
who	have	little	want

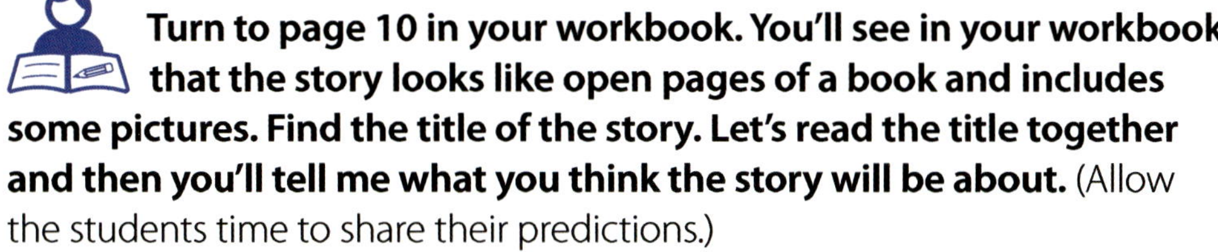

Reading

READ A STORY

Now, let's read a story.

Turn to page 10 in your workbook. You'll see in your workbook that the story looks like open pages of a book and includes some pictures. Find the title of the story. Let's read the title together and then you'll tell me what you think the story will be about. (Allow the students time to share their predictions.)

Now, find the first sentence of the story. Here are the steps:
1. Look at each word and decide if it's a high-frequency word.
   - If it's a high-frequency word, read the word.
   - If it's not a high-frequency word, point to the letters, say the sounds, and then read the word.
2. Use this routine to read all the sentences in the story.
3. After you read the story, we will read it together.

Fed in Bed

The sun is up.
Ken, Sis, and Dad are up.
Mom is not up yet.
Now Ken, Sis, and Dad have a job.
Sis has a cup.
Ken has a bun and jam.
Dad has a hot pan.
They mix and they fix.
What a good job.
Ken, Sis, and Dad fed Mom in bed.

(After reading, ask students who made Mom breakfast. **Her family made her breakfast.**)

Day
7

Writing

WRITE SENTENCES

Now we'll practice writing sentences. The first word in a sentence starts with an uppercase letter, and there's a punctuation mark at the end like a period or question mark.

Answer with me as we do the first one together.

Let's write the following sentence: The sun is hot. Repeat it with me.
The sun is hot. (Hold up 1 finger for each word as you repeat the sentence.)
- **How many words do you hear? 4**
- **What is the first word? The I write the high-frequency word spelled uppercase T, lowercase h-e.**
- (Repeat the sentence.) **What is the second word? sun**
  - **Sounds and letters? /s/ s - /ŭ/ u - /n/ n**
- (Repeat the sentence.) **What is the third word? is I write the high-frequency word spelled i-s.**
- (Repeat the sentence.) **What is the next word? hot**
  - **Sounds and letters? /h/ h - /ŏ/ o - /t/ t**
- **Punctuation mark? period**
- **Read the sentence. The sun is hot.**

 Now it's your turn. Turn to page 14 in your Student Workbook. Find the line that has a key in front of it.

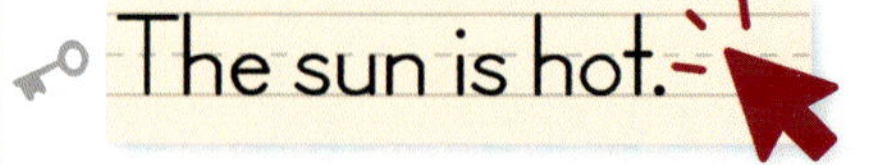

(Display word box.)
Above the line, there is a box that has some high-frequency words that we have learned. Let's read them together. **jump, are, this**

jump, are, this

Here are the steps:
1. I'll say the sentence and you repeat it.
2. I'll say each word, and before you write it, decide if it's a high-frequency word. Use the word boxes in your workbook to help you.
   - If it's a high-frequency word, write the letters.
   - If it's not a high-frequency word, break the word into sounds and write the letter for each sound.
3. Make sure the first letter in your sentence is uppercase.
4. Put a punctuation mark at the end.
5. Then, read the sentence.

1. Jump in and get wet.
2. They are wet.
3. This is fun.

Now that you have written 3 sentences, go back to the top and trace the first sentence. Finally, whisper read all 4 sentences.

Day **7**

Phonological Awareness Wrap-Up

PHONOLOGICAL AWARENESS: BLENDING 2-PHONEME WORDS

Today we are going to practice <u>blending 2 sounds</u> to say a word.
Let's review the instructions:
- I'll say the sounds.
- Then, I'll ask you to tell me the word. Ready?

/oi/ /l/: Word?	oil	/l/ /ā/: Word?	lay
/ĭ/ /l/: Word?	ill	/l/ /ō/: Word?	low
/w/ /ā/: Word?	way	/r/ /ā/: Word?	ray
/n/ /ō/: Word?	no	/ō/ /t/: Word?	oat
/f/ /or/: Word?	for	/s/ /ū/: Word?	Sue
/ă/ /n/: Word?	an	/m/ /ā/: Word?	may
/ī/ /s/: Word?	ice	/ā/ /j/: Word?	age
/ĭ/ /n/: Word?	in	/d/ /ā/: Word?	day

DAY 8

Phonological Awareness Warm-Up

PHONOLOGICAL AWARENESS: BLENDING 2- AND 3-PHONEME WORDS

Today we are going to practice <u>blending 2 or 3 sounds</u> to say a word.
Let's review the instructions:
- I'll say the sounds.
- Then, I'll ask you to tell me the word. Ready?

/n/ /ō/ /t/: Word?	note	/m/ /ŭ/ /ch/: Word?	much
/r/ /ŭ/ /b/: Word?	rub	/l/ /ă/ /p/: Word?	lap
/d/ /ĭ/ /sh/: Word?	dish	/n/ /ĭ/ /p/: Word?	nip
/sh/ /ē/: Word?	she	/sh/ /ō/: Word?	show
/k/ /ă/ /t/: Word?	cat	/n/ /ī/ /t/: Word?	night
/h/ /ĭ/ /m/: Word?	him	/k/ /ē/: Word?	key
/r/ /ĭ/ /d/: Word?	rid	/r/ /ō/ /d/: Word?	rode
/ŭ/ /p/: Word?	up	/l/ /ă/ /sh/: Word?	lash

Letter-Sound Correspondence

WORD COMPLETION WITH PICTURES

Now we're going to fill in the missing sounds in words. Look at each picture. Fill in the correct letter to complete the word. After you write the letter, whisper read the word.

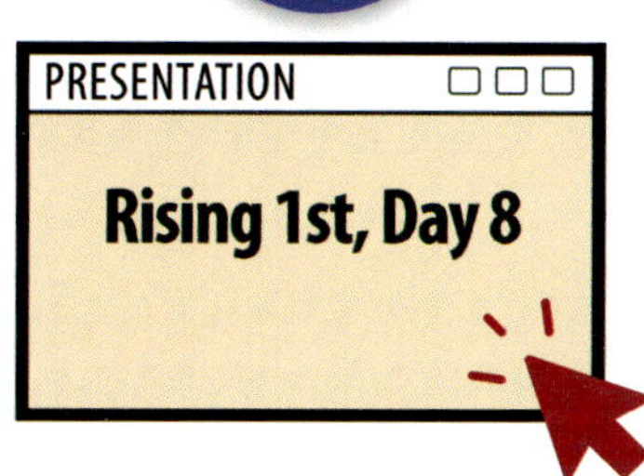

(Display <u>cap</u>.)
I'll do the first one. This picture is <u>cap</u>.
- **I finger-stretch cap. /k/ /ă/ /p/**
- **I tap the letters and line while saying the sounds to see what sound is missing.** (Tap the line, the letter *a*, and the letter *p*.)
  - **The first sound /k/ is missing. In this word, the sound /k/ is spelled with the letter *c*.**
- **Next, I write the letter *c* in the space.**
- **Finally, I slide a finger under the word and whisper "cap."**

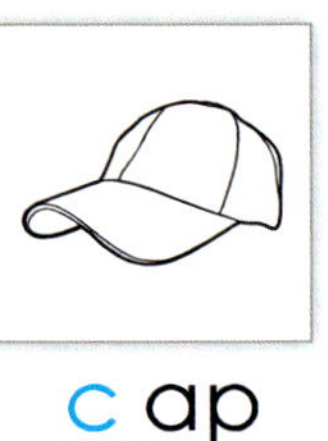

 **Now it's your turn. Turn to page 14 in your Student Workbook.** (Review the name of each picture with students before they begin.)

Here are the steps:
1. **Finger-stretch the sounds.**
2. **Tap the letters and line while saying the sounds.**
3. **Write the letter for the missing sound.**
4. **Whisper read the word.**

Answer Key

High-Frequency Words

Now I'm going to show you how to read 4 more high-frequency words. Watch me, my turn.

(Display <u>be</u>.)
The word is <u>be</u>, as in the sentence "Will you be at the party?"
- **Watch me finger-stretch the sounds. /b/ /ē/** (Show thumb for /b/ and pointer finger for /ē/.)
- **There are 2 sounds in the word *be*. This word is spelled with 2 letters, *b-e*.**

Now it's your turn. Word? be How many letters? 2
The letter names are b-e. Say them with me. b-e

(Use the process below to review the next 3 words.)

HFW List	
he /h/ /ē/	• **The word is ______. What is the word?** ______ • **Listen for this word in the following sentence.** (Use the word in a sentence.) • **Watch me finger-stretch the sounds.** • **There are** (number) **sound(s) in the word** ______. • **This word is spelled with** (number) **letter(s),** ______.
me /m/ /ē/	**Now it's your turn.**
we /w/ /ē/	• **Word?** ______ **How many letter(s)?** ______ • **The letter name(s) are** ______. **Say them with me.** ______

How are the words *be,* *he,* *me,* **and** *we* **alike?** (answers vary: **They all end in the sound /ē/. They all end with the letter** *e.* **They rhyme.**)

FLUENCY: HIGH-FREQUENCY WORDS

Now we will practice reading the words we know.

(Display the high-frequency word grid. Prompt students by saying **"Word?"** at each box.)

me	we	he	be
this	are	good	jump
what	down	has	have
come	now	they	little

Reading

READ SENTENCES

It's sentence time!

Turn to page 15 in your workbook. Find the line that has a plane in front of it.

(Display word box.)
Above the line, there is a box with some high-frequency words that we have learned. Let's read them together. we, me, he Now, put your pointer finger in front of the first word in the sentence.

(Display sentence.)
Answer with me as we read the first sentence together.
- **How many words do you see? 3**
- **How is the first word spelled? uppercase G-u-s**
  - **First sound? /g/ Next sound? /ŭ/ Last sound? /s/ Word? Gus**
  - **Notice that G is an uppercase letter because it is the first word in the sentence and it is the first letter of a name.**

Note: Stop to chorally read the 16 words in the long box at the top of the workbook pages. Doing this at least once a day can help to build automaticity of these high-frequency words.

we, me, he

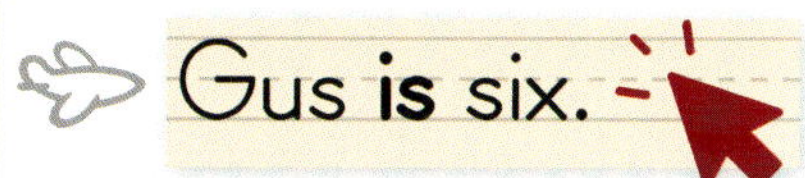

Day
8

- **How is the second word spelled? i-s** This is the bold high-frequency word *is*.
- **How is the third word spelled? s-i-x**
  - **First sound? /s/ Next sound? /ĭ/ Last sounds? /k/ /s/ Word? six**
- **Which punctuation mark is at the end? a period**
- **Now read the sentence. Gus is six.**

Now it's your turn. On the line that has a plane in front of it, find the sentence that is next to the one we just read together. Put your pointer finger in front of the first word.

Let's review the steps:
1. **Put your finger under each word.**
   - **If the word is bold, it's a high-frequency word. Read the word.**
   - **If it's not a high-frequency word, point to the letters, say the sounds, and then read the word.**
2. **Continue until you read each word.**
3. **Then read the sentence.**

(After reading the sentences, ask the students who said "Look at me"? **Gus said "Look at me."** Yes, we know Gus said "Look at me" because there are quotation marks around it.)

> 1. **We see** him bat.
> 2. Gus **said,** "**Look** at **me**."
> 3. **He** had **a** big hit.

Writing

WRITE SENTENCES

Now we'll practice writing sentences. Remember, the first word in a sentence starts with an uppercase letter, and there's a punctuation mark at the end like a period or question mark.

Answer with me as we do the first one together.

Let's write the following sentence: We want to be fit. Repeat it with me. **We want to be fit.** (Hold up 1 finger for each word as you repeat the sentence.)
- **How many words do you hear? 5**
- (Repeat the sentence.) **What is the first word? We** I write the high-frequency word *we*.
  - **Notice that W is uppercase because it's the first word in a sentence.**
- (Repeat the sentence.) **What is the second word? want** I write the high-frequency word *want*.
- (Repeat the sentence.) **What is the third word? to** I write the high-frequency word *to*.

Day
8

- (Repeat the sentence.) **What is the fourth word? be** I write the high-frequency word *be.*
- (Repeat the sentence.) **What is the last word? fit**
  - **Sounds and letters? /f/ f - /ĭ/ i - /t/ t**
- **Punctuation mark? period**
- **Read the sentence. We want to be fit.**

 **Now it's your turn. Turn to page 15 in your Student Workbook. Find the line that has a crown in front of it.**

(Display word box.)

Above the line, there is a box that has some high-frequency words that we have learned. Let's read them together. **we, he, me, I**

Here are the steps:

1. **I'll say the sentence and you repeat it.**
2. **I'll say each word, and before you write it, decide if it's a high-frequency word. Use the word boxes in your workbook to help you.**
   - **If it's a high-frequency word, write the letters.**
   - **If it's not a high-frequency word, break the word into sounds and write the letter for each sound.**
3. **Make sure the first letter in your sentence is uppercase.**
4. **Put a punctuation mark at the end.**
5. **Then, read the sentence.**

Now that you have written 3 sentences, go back to the top and trace the first sentence. Finally, whisper read all 4 sentences.

we, he, me, I

1. We run a lap.
2. He can hop to me.
3. I can hop to him.

Phonological Awareness Wrap-Up

PHONOLOGICAL AWARENESS: BLENDING 2- AND 3-PHONEME WORDS

Today we are going to practice blending 2 or 3 sounds to say a word. Let's review the instructions:

- **I'll say the sounds.**
- **Then, I'll ask you to tell me the word. Ready?**

/ă/ /d/: Word?	add	/k/ /yū/ /t/: Word?	cute
/k/ /ā/ /j/: Word?	cage	/l/ /ō/: Word?	low
/g/ /ō/: Word?	go	/z/ /ă/ /p/: Word?	zap
/f/ /ĕ/ /d/: Word?	fed	/w/ /ĕ/ /b/: Word?	web
/ou/ /t/: Word?	out	/l/ /ŏ/ /g/: Word?	log
/sh/ /ĕ/ /d/: Word?	shed	/w/ /ā/ /d/: Word?	wade
/h/ /ī/ /v/: Word?	hive	/m/ /ē/: Word?	me
/v/ /ā/ /s/: Word?	vase	/hw/ /ĕ/ /n/: Word?	when

Day
9

DAY 9

Phonological Awareness Warm-Up

PHONOLOGICAL AWARENESS: BLENDING 2- AND 3-PHONEME WORDS

**Today we are going to practice <u>blending 2 or 3 sounds</u> to say a word.
Let's review the instructions:**
- **I'll say the sounds.**
- **Then, I'll ask you to tell me the word. Ready?**

/r/ /ĭ/ /ch/: Word?	rich	/f/ /ā/ /s/: Word?	face
/y/ /ĕ/ /t/: Word?	yet	/p/ /ā/: Word?	pay
/f/ /ā/ /d/: Word?	fade	/h/ /ī/ /k/: Word?	hike
/b/ /ā/: Word?	bay	/p/ /ŭ/ /p/: Word?	pup
/h/ /ĕ/ /n/: Word?	hen	/g/ /ā/ /v/: Word?	gave
/d/ /ē/ /p/: Word?	deep	/k/ /ŭ/ /p/: Word?	cup
/r/ /ō/ /z/: Word?	rose	/m/ /ŭ/ /d/: Word?	mud
/ĭ/ /f/: Word?	if	/j/ /ĕ/ /l/: Word?	gel

High-Frequency Words

**Now I'm going to show you how to read 4 more high-frequency words.
Watch me, my turn.**

(Display <u>find</u>.)
The word is <u>find</u>, as in the sentence "We will find the treasure."
- **Watch me finger-stretch the sounds. /f/ /ī/ /n/ /d/** (Show thumb for /f/, pointer finger for /ī/, middle finger for /n/, and ring finger for /d/.)
- **There are 4 sounds in the word *find*. This word is spelled with 4 letters, *f-i-n-d*.**

**Now it's your turn. Word? find How many letters? 4
The letter names are f-i-n-d. Say them with me. f-i-n-d**

(Use the process below to review the next 3 words.)

HFW List	
day /d/ /ā/	• **The word is _______. What is the word? _______** • **Listen for this word in the following sentence.** (Use the word in a sentence.) • **Watch me finger-stretch the sounds.** • **There are** <u>(number)</u> **sound(s) in the word _______.** • **This word is spelled with** <u>(number)</u> **letter(s), _______.** **Now it's your turn.** • **Word? _______ How many letter(s)? _______** • **The letter name(s) are _______. Say them with me. _______**
play /p/ /l/ /ā/	
say /s/ /ā/	

How are the words *day*, *play*, and *say* alike? (answers vary: **They all end in the sound /ā/. They all end with the letters a-y. They rhyme.**)

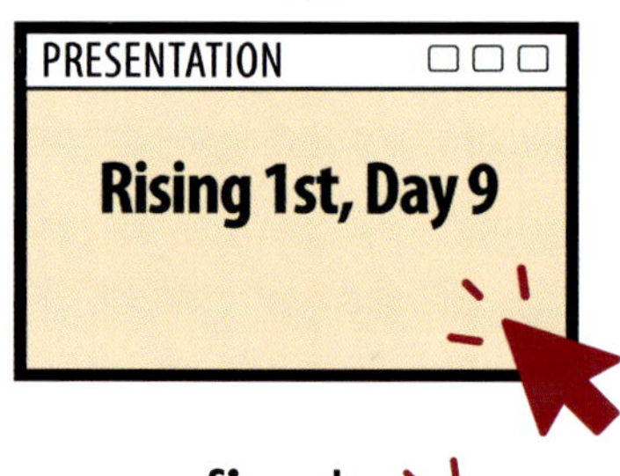

PRESENTATION

Rising 1st, Day 9

find

day
play
say

FLUENCY: HIGH-FREQUENCY WORDS

Now we will practice reading the words we know.

(Display the high-frequency word grid. Prompt students by saying **"Word?"** at each box.)

say	day	find	play
be	are	down	has
good	he	me	jump
have	what	this	we

Reading

READ A STORY

Now we will reread the story, *Fed in Bed*.

 **Turn to page 10 in your workbook. Find the title of the story. Let's read it together. Fed in Bed**

Now, find the first sentence of the story. Here are the steps:
1. **Look at each word and decide if it's a high-frequency word.**
   - **If it's a high-frequency word, read the word.**
   - **If it's not a high-frequency word, point to the letters, say the sounds, and then read the word.**
2. **Continue until you read each word in the story.**

We'll discuss the story when you've finished reading.

Fed in Bed
The sun is up.
Ken, Sis, and Dad are up.
Mom is not up yet.
Now Ken, Sis, and Dad have a job.
Sis has a cup.
Ken has a bun and jam.
Dad has a hot pan.
They mix and they fix.
What a good job.
Ken, Sis, and Dad fed Mom in bed.

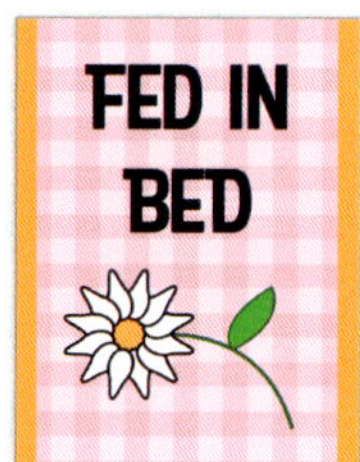

(After reading, ask students where Mom ate breakfast. **Mom ate in bed.**)

Writing

WRITE SENTENCES

Now we'll practice writing sentences. The first word in a sentence starts with an uppercase letter, and there's a punctuation mark at the end like a period or question mark.

Answer with me as we do the first one together.

Let's write the following sentence: <u>We can play.</u> Repeat it with me.
We can play. (Hold up 1 finger for each word as you repeat the sentence.)
- **How many words do you hear? 3**
- (Repeat the sentence.) **What is the first word? We I write the high-frequency word spelled uppercase W, lowercase e.**
  - **Notice that W is uppercase because it's the first word In a sentence.**
- (Repeat the sentence.) **What is the second word? can**
  - **Sounds and letters? /k/ c - /ă/ a - /n/ n**
- (Repeat the sentence.) **What is the third word? play I write the high-frequency word spelled p-l-a-y.**
- **Punctuation mark? period**
- **Read the sentence. We can play.**

 Now it's your turn. Turn to page 16 in your Student Workbook. Find the line that has a truck in front of it.

(Display word box.)
Above the line, there is a box that has some high-frequency words that we have learned. Let's read them together. **find, me, I**

Here are the steps:
1. I'll say the sentence and you repeat it.
2. I'll say each word, and before you write it, decide if it's a high-frequency word. Use the word boxes in your workbook to help you.
   - If it's a high-frequency word, write the letters.
   - If it's not a high-frequency word, break the word into sounds and write the letter for each sound.
3. Make sure the first letter in your sentence is uppercase.
4. Put a punctuation mark at the end.
5. Then, read the sentence.

Now that you have written 3 sentences, go back to the top and trace the first sentence. Finally, whisper read all 4 sentences.

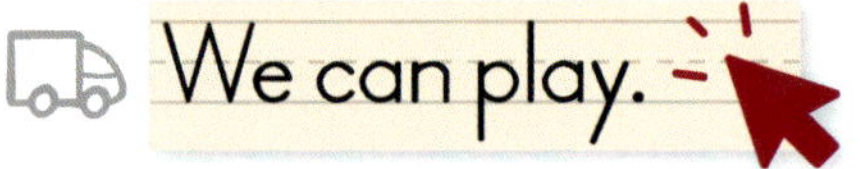

find, me, I

1. Come find me.
2. I hid in the hut.
3. Can you see me?

Day
9

Phonological Awareness Wrap-Up

PHONOLOGICAL AWARENESS: BLENDING 2- AND 3-PHONEME WORDS

Today we are going to practice blending 2 or 3 sounds to say a word. Let's review the instructions:
- I'll say the sounds.
- Then, I'll ask you to tell me the word. Ready?

/r/ /ĭ/ /b/: Word?	rib	/z/ /ō/ /n/: Word?	zone
/f/ /ĭ/ /n/: Word?	fin	/v/ /ĕ/ /t/: Word?	vet
/s/ /ŭ/ /n/: Word?	sun	/j/ /ă/ /m/: Word?	jam
/b/ /ē/ /p/: Word?	beep	/z/ /ū/: Word?	zoo
/k/ /ā/ /j/: Word?	cage	/s/ /ō/: Word?	so
/d/ /ā/ /t/: Word?	date	/f/ /ī/ /n/: Word?	fine
/j/ /ā/: Word?	jay	/r/ /ĕ/ /d/: Word?	red
/ch/ /ă/ /t/: Word?	chat	/d/ /ĭ/ /g/: Word?	dig

DAY 10

Phonological Awareness Warm-Up

PHONOLOGICAL AWARENESS: BLENDING 3-PHONEME WORDS

Today we are going to practice blending 3 sounds to say a word. Let's review the instructions:
- I'll say the sounds.
- Then, I'll ask you to tell me the word. Ready?

/t/ /ū/ /n/: Word?	tune	/ĭ/ /n/ /ch/: Word?	inch
/ĭ/ /t/ /s/: Word?	it's	/l/ /ĭ/ /d/: Word?	lid
/m/ /ā/ /d/: Word?	maid	/ch/ /ŏ/ /p/: Word?	chop
/s/ /ā/ /l/: Word?	sail	/d/ /ĭ/ /d/: Word?	did
/b/ /ē/ /f/: Word?	beef	/p/ /ă/ /k/: Word?	pack
/j/ /ŏ/ /g/: Word?	jog	/d/ /ă/ /sh/: Word?	dash
/g/ /ō/ /t/: Word?	goat	/b/ /ŏ/ /b/: Word?	bob
/sh/ /ĭ/ /p/: Word?	ship	/p/ /ā/ /l/: Word?	pail

Letter-Sound Correspondence

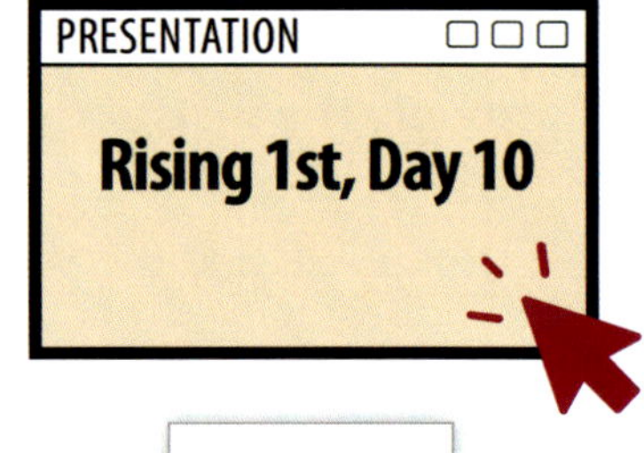
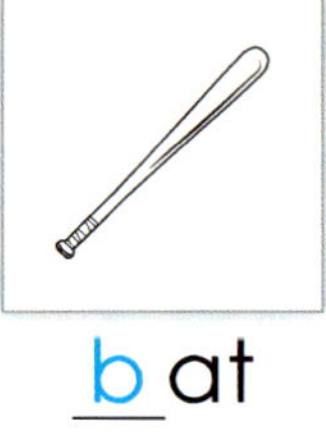

WORD COMPLETION WITH PICTURES

Now we're going to fill in the missing sound in words. Look at each picture. Fill in the correct letter to complete the word. After you write the letter, whisper read the word.

I'll do the first one. This picture is <u>bat</u>.
- I finger-stretch bat. /b/ /ă/ /t/
- I tap the letters and line while saying the sounds to see what sound is missing. (Tap the line, the letter *a*, and the letter *t*.)
  - The first sound /b/ is missing. The sound /b/ is spelled with the letter *b*.
- Next, I write the letter *b* in the space.
- Finally, I slide a finger under the word and whisper "bat."

 **Now it's your turn. Turn to page 17 in your Student Workbook.** (Review the name of each picture with students before they begin.)

Here are the steps:
1. Finger-stretch the sounds.
2. Tap the letters and line while saying the sounds.
3. Write the letter for the missing sound.
4. Whisper read the word.

Answer Key

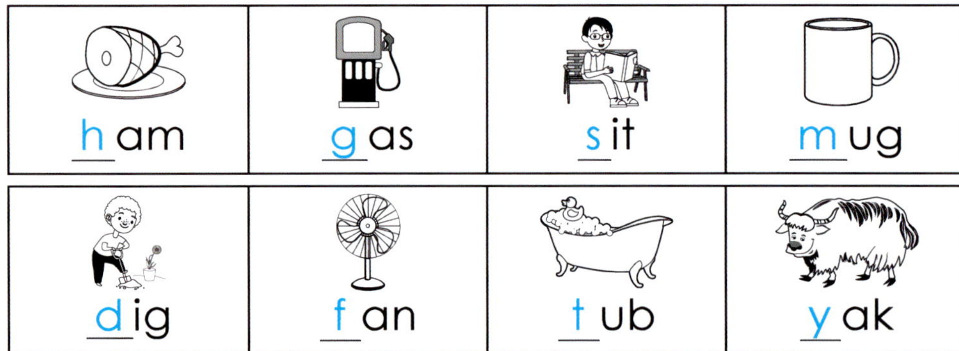

h am	g as	s it	m ug
d ig	f an	t ub	y ak

Day
10

High-Frequency Words

Now I'm going to show you how to read 4 more high-frequency words. Watch me, my turn.

(Display <u>away</u>.)

The word is <u>away</u>, as in the sentence "The bird flew away."

- **Watch me finger-stretch the sounds. /ə/ /w/ /ā/** (Show thumb for /ə/, pointer finger for /w/, and middle finger for /ā/.)
- **There are 3 sounds in the word** *away*. **This word is spelled with 4 letters,** *a-w-a-y*.

Now it's your turn. Word? away How many letters? 4
The letter names are a-w-a-y. Say them with me. a-w-a-y

(Use the process below to review the next 3 words.)

Note: The schwa sound, which is a reduced vowel sound, is noted with the upside down e, (/ə/). The schwa sound in the word *away*, sounds like the reduced short u vowel sound.

his
that
with

HFW List	
his /h/ /ĭ/ /z/	• **The word is _______. What is the word? _______** • **Listen for this word in the following sentence.** (Use the word in a sentence.) • **Watch me finger-stretch the sounds.** • **There are** (number) **sound(s) in the word _______.** • **This word is spelled with** (number) **letter(s), _______.** **Now it's your turn.** • **Word? _______ How many letter(s)? _______** • **The letter name(s) are _______. Say them with me. _______**
that /<u>th</u>/ /ă/ /t/	
with /w/ /ĭ/ /<u>th</u>/	

FLUENCY: HIGH-FREQUENCY WORDS

Now we will practice reading the words we know.

(Display the high-frequency word grid. Prompt students by saying **"Word?"** at each box.)

that	away	with	his
find	play	day	he
me	be	good	jump
are	say	we	this

Day
10

Reading

READ SENTENCES

It's sentence time!

Turn to page 17 in your workbook and find the line that has a high-top shoe in front of it.

(Display word box.)

Above the line, there is a box with some high-frequency words that we have learned. Let's read them together. his, he, away, we, with

his, he, away, we, with

Now, put your pointer finger in front of the first word in the sentence.

(Display sentence.)

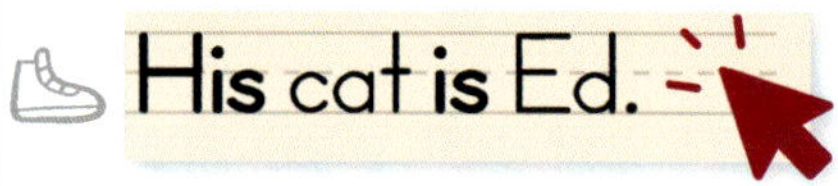

Let's read the first sentence together. (Follow the same process from previous days. Read the bold high-frequency words and sound out the decodable words that are not bold.)

Now it's your turn. On the line that has a high-top shoe in front of it, find the sentence that is next to the one we just read together. Put your pointer finger in front of the first word.

1. Did **he** run **away**?
2. **We** can **look for** him.
3. **He is** at **the** vet **with** Mom.

Let's review the steps:
1. **Put your finger under each word.**
   - **If the word is bold, it's a high-frequency word. Read the word.**
   - **If it's not a high-frequency word, point to the letters, say the sounds, and then read the word.**
2. **Continue until you read each word.**
3. **Then read the sentence.**

(After reading, ask the students what the cat's name is. **The cat's name is Ed.**)

Writing

WRITE SENTENCES

Now we'll practice writing sentences.

Answer with me as we do the first one together.

Let's write the following sentence: I am ten. Repeat it with me. I am ten.
(Hold up 1 finger for each word as you repeat the sentence.)
- **How many words do you hear?** 3
- (Repeat the sentence.) **What is the first word?** I I write the high-frequency word spelled uppercase I.
   - **Notice that I is uppercase because it's the first word in a sentence. Also, the high-frequency word *I* is always uppercase no matter where it appears in a sentence.**
- (Repeat the sentence.) **What is the second word?** am

 95 Phonics Booster Bundle™: Summer School Edition 2021 • Rising First • Teacher's Edition

- – **Sounds and letters?** **/ă/ a - /m/ m**
- (Repeat the sentence.) **What is the last word? ten**
  - – **Sounds and letters?** **/t/ t- /ĕ/ e - /n/ n**
- **Punctuation mark? period**
- **Read the sentence. I am ten.**

 Now it's your turn. Turn to page 18 in your Student Workbook. Find the line that has scissors in front of it.

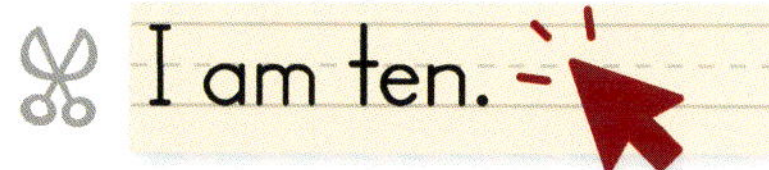

(Display word box.)

Above the line, there is a box that has some high-frequency words that we have learned. Let's read them together. **I, good, play, with, my**

I, good, play, with, my

Here are the steps:
1. I'll say the sentence and you repeat it.
2. I'll say each word, and before you write it, decide if it's a high-frequency word. Use the word boxes in your workbook to help you.
   - If it's a high-frequency word, write the letters.
   - If it's not a high-frequency word, break the word into sounds and write the letter for each sound.
3. Make sure the first letter in your sentence is uppercase.
4. Put a punctuation mark at the end.
5. Then, read the sentence.

1. I am a good kid.
2. I play with my dog.
3. Want to play with us?

Now that you have written 3 sentences, go back to the top and trace the first sentence. Finally, whisper read all 4 sentences.

Phonological Awareness Wrap-Up

PHONOLOGICAL AWARENESS: BLENDING 3-PHONEME WORDS

Today we are going to practice blending 3 sounds to say a word. Let's review the instructions:
- I'll say the sounds.
- Then, I'll ask you to tell me the word. Ready?

/s/ /ă/ /d/: Word?	sad	/j/ /ō/ /k/: Word?	joke
/hw/ /ă/ /m/: Word?	wham	/z/ /ĭ/ /p/: Word?	zip
/t/ /ū/ /b/: Word?	tube	/h/ /ō/ /l/: Word?	hole
/l/ /ĕ/ /g/: Word?	leg	/b/ /ā/ /k/: Word?	bake
/m/ /ŭ/ /g/: Word?	mug	/j/ /ĭ/ /g/: Word?	jig
/k/ /ĭ/ /s/: Word?	kiss	/g/ /ā/ /n/: Word?	gain
/ch/ /ĭ/ /n/: Word?	chin	/h/ /ŏ/ /p/: Word?	hop
/m/ /ă/ /th/: Word?	math	/w/ /ĭ/ /n/: Word?	win

Day 11

Days 11–15: Short Vowels, Reading, & Writing 2

Learning Objective

Students demonstrate understanding of how to read sentences and short stories with decodable VC and CVC words and selected irregularly spelled high-frequency words. Additionally, they write short sentences composed of these types of words.

DAY 11

Phonological Awareness Warm-Up

PHONOLOGICAL AWARENESS: PHONEME SEGMENTATION

Today we are going to practice <u>segmenting sounds</u> in words with 2 sounds.

Listen, my turn.
The word is <u>at</u>. I finger-stretch while saying each sound in the word.
/ă/ /t/ (Remember, finger-stretch from right to left, starting with your thumb.)

Let's practice.
- Say <u>it</u>: (it) Finger-stretch and say the sounds in the word *it*. /ĭ/ /t/
- Say <u>up</u>: (up) Sounds? /ŭ/ /p/

Now it's your turn. Here are the instructions:
- I'll say a word and you repeat it.
- Then, I'll tell you to segment, or say, all the sounds in the word. Ready?

Say as: (as) Sounds?	/ă/ /z/	Say show: (show) Sounds?	/sh/ /ō/
Say no: (no) Sounds?	/n/ /ō/	Say to: (to) Sounds?	/t/ /ū/
Say app: (app) Sounds?	/ă/ /p/	Say am: (am) Sounds?	/ă/ /m/
Say shoe: (shoe) Sounds?	/sh/ /ū/	Say in: (in) Sounds?	/ĭ/ /n/
Say if: (if) Sounds?	/ĭ/ /f/	Say my: (my) Sounds?	/m/ /ī/
Say we: (we) Sounds?	/w/ /ē/	Say go: (go) Sounds?	/g/ /ō/
Say us: (us) Sounds?	/ŭ/ /s/	Say eat: (eat) Sounds?	/ē/ /t/
Say me: (me) Sounds?	/m/ /ē/	Say an: (an) Sounds?	/ă/ /n/

Day
11

Letter-Sound Correspondence

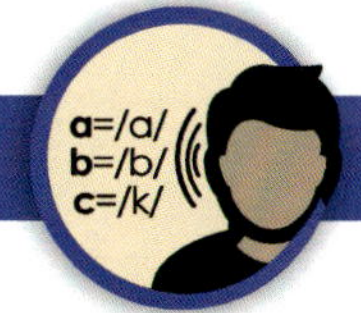

WORD COMPLETION WITH PICTURES

Now we're going to fill in the missing sound in words. Look at each picture. Fill in the correct letter to complete the word. After you write the letter, whisper read the word.

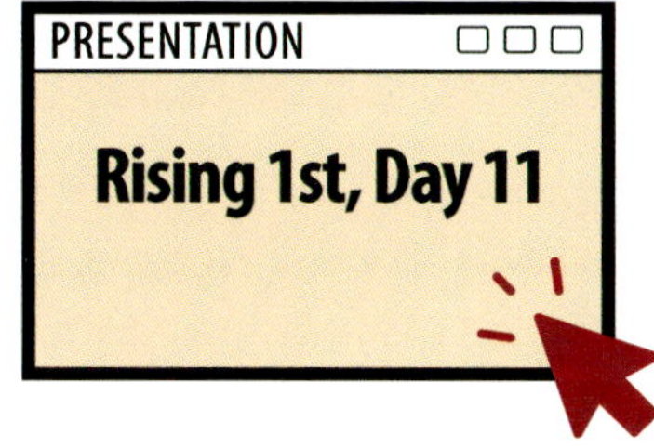

(Display <u>hot</u>.)
I'll do the first one. This picture is <u>hot</u>.
- I finger-stretch hot. /h/ /ŏ/ /t/
- I tap the letters and line while saying the sounds to see what sound is missing. (Tap the letter *h*, the letter *o*, and the line.)
  - **The last sound /t/ is missing. The sound /t/ is spelled with the letter *t*.**
- **Next, I write the letter *t* in the space.**
- **Finally, I slide a finger under the word and whisper "hot."**

ho<u>t</u>

 **Now it's your turn. Turn to page 21 in your Student Workbook.** (Review the name of each picture with students before they begin.)

Here are the steps:
1. **Finger-stretch the sounds.**
2. **Tap the letters and line while saying the sounds.**
3. **Write the letter for the missing sound.**
4. **Whisper read the word.**

Answer Key

Day 11

High-Frequency Words

Now I'm going to show you how to read 4 more high-frequency words. Watch me, my turn.

(Display go.)
The word is go, as in the sentence "Let's go to the park."
- **Watch me finger-stretch the sounds. /g/ /ō/** (Show thumb for /g/ and pointer finger for /ō/.)
- **There are 2 sounds in the word go. This word is spelled with 2 letters, g-o.**

Now it's your turn. Word? go How many letters? 2
The letter names are g-o. Say them with me. g-o

(Use the process below to review the next 3 words.)

go

HFW List	
no /n/ /ō/	• **The word is _______. What is the word? _______** • **Listen for this word in the following sentence.** (Use the word in a sentence.) • **Watch me finger-stretch the sounds.** • **There are** (number) **sound(s) in the word _______.** • **This word is spelled with** (number) **letter(s), _______.**
so /s/ /ō/	**Now it's your turn.**
yes /y/ /ĕ/ /s/	• **Word? _______ How many letter(s)? _______** • **The letter name(s) are _______. Say them with me. _______**

no
so
yes

How are the words go, no, and so alike? (answers vary: **They all end in the /ō/ sound. They all end in the letter o. They rhyme.**)

FLUENCY: HIGH-FREQUENCY WORDS

Now we will practice reading the words we know.

(Display the high-frequency word grid. Prompt students by saying **"Word?"** at each box.)

so	go	yes	no
his	find	he	away
day	be	with	say
we	that	play	me

Reading

cat

READ SENTENCES

It's sentence time!

Turn to page 22 in your workbook. Find the line that has a rocket in front of it.

(Display word box.)
Above the line, there is a box with some high-frequency words that we have learned. Let's read them together. we, jump, yes, so, I, with, down, go

we, jump, yes, so, I,
with, down, go

Now, put your pointer finger in front of the first word in the sentence.

(Display sentence.)
Let's read the first sentence together. (Follow the same process from previous days. Read the bold high-frequency words and sound out the decodable words that are not bold.)

Can **we jump** on **the** bed?

Now it's your turn. On the line that has a rocket in front of it, find the sentence that is next to the one we just read together. Put your pointer finger in front of the first word.

Let's review the steps:
1. **Look at each word and decide if it's a high-frequency word.**
   - **If the word is bold, it's a high-frequency word. Read the word.**
   - **If it's not a high-frequency word, point to the letters, say the sounds, and then read the word.**
2. **Continue until you read each word.**
3. **Then read the sentence.**

1. Ben **said yes.**
2. **So I jump with** Ben.
3. But **down we go.**

(After reading, point out that these 4 sentences tell a story. Ask what happened when they jumped on the bed. **They fell down.**)

Writing

WRITE SENTENCES

Now we'll practice writing sentences.

Answer with me as we do the first one together.

Let's write the following sentence: Jen and Lin are sad. **Repeat it with me.** Jen and Lin are sad. (Hold up 1 finger for each word as you repeat the sentence.)

- **How many words do you hear?** 5
- **What is the first word?** Jen **Remember, the first word in a sentence and the first letter of a name are uppercase.**
  - **Say the sounds and letters.** /j/ uppercase J - /ĕ/ e - /n/ n
- (Repeat the sentence.) **What is the second word?** and **This high-frequency word is spelled a-n-d.**
- (Repeat the sentence.) **What is the third word?** Lin **This is name so it begins with an uppercase letter.**
  - **Say the sounds and letters.** /l/ uppercase L - /ĭ/ i - /n/ n
- (Repeat the sentence.) **What is the fourth word?** are **This high-frequency word is spelled a-r-e.**
- (Repeat the sentence.) **What is the last word?** sad
  - **Say the sounds and letters.** /s/ s - /ă/ a - /d/ d
- **Punctuation mark?** period
- **Read the sentence.** Jen and Lin are sad.

 **Now it's your turn. Turn to page 22 in your Student Workbook. Find the line that has an umbrella in front of it.**

(Display word box.)

Above the line, there is a box that has some high-frequency words that we have learned. Let's read them together. this, go, no

Here are the steps:
1. **I'll say the sentence and you repeat it.**
2. **I'll say each word, and before you write it, decide if it's a high-frequency word. Use the word boxes in your workbook to help you.**
   - **If it's a high-frequency word, write the letters.**
   - **If it's not a high-frequency word, break the word into sounds and write the letter for each sound.**
3. **Make sure the first letter in your sentence and all names are uppercase.**
4. **Put a punctuation mark at the end.**
5. **Then, read the sentence.**

Now that you have written 3 sentences, go back to the top and trace the first sentence. Finally, whisper read all 4 sentences.

this, go, no

1. This is bad.
2. They want to go.
3. But Dad said no.

Day
11

Phonological Awareness Wrap-Up

PHONOLOGICAL AWARENESS: PHONEME SEGMENTATION

Today we are going to practice <u>segmenting sounds</u> in words with 2 sounds.

Let's practice.
- **Say <u>me</u>: (me)** Finger-stretch and say the sounds in the word *me*. **/m/ /ē/**
- **Say <u>key</u>: (key)** Sounds? **/k/ /ē/**

Now it's your turn. Let's review the instructions:
- **I'll say a word and you repeat it.**
- **Then, I'll tell you to segment, or say, all the sounds in the word. Ready?**

Say on: (on) Sounds?	/ŏ/ /n/	Say use: (use) Sounds?	/yū/ /z/
Say row: (row) Sounds?	/r/ /ō/	Say see: (see) Sounds?	/s/ /ē/
Say add: (add) Sounds?	/ă/ /d/	Say ash: (ash) Sounds?	/ă/ /sh/
Say ray: (ray) Sounds?	/r/ /ā/	Say of: (of) Sounds?	/ŭ/ /v/
Say hi: (hi) Sounds?	/h/ /ī/	Say knee: (knee) Sounds?	/n/ /ē/
Say do: (do) Sounds?	/d/ /ū/	Say she: (she) Sounds?	/sh/ /ē/
Say so: (so) Sounds?	/s/ /ō/	Say chew: (chew) Sounds?	/ch/ /ū/
Say ate: (ate) Sounds?	/ā/ /t/	Say may: (may) Sounds?	/m/ /ā/

DAY 12

Phonological Awareness Warm-Up

PHONOLOGICAL AWARENESS: PHONEME SEGMENTATION

Today we are going to practice <u>segmenting sounds</u> in words with 2 sounds.

Let's practice.
- **Say <u>my</u>: (my)** Sounds? **/m/ /ī/**

Now it's your turn. Let's review the instructions:
- **I'll say a word and you repeat it.**
- **Then, I'll tell you to segment, or say, all the sounds in the word. Ready?**

Say to: (to) Sounds?	/t/ /ū/	Say why: (why) Sounds?	/hw/ /ī/
Say tea: (tea) Sounds?	/t/ /ē/	Say new: (new) Sounds?	/n/ /ū/
Say it: (it) Sounds?	/ĭ/ /t/	Say he: (he) Sounds?	/h/ /ē/
Say ape: (ape) Sounds?	/ā/ /p/	Say up: (up) Sounds?	/ŭ/ /p/
Say boo: (boo) Sounds?	/b/ /ū/	Say high: (high) Sounds?	/h/ /ī/
Say pie: (pie) Sounds?	/p/ /ī/	Say hay: (hay) Sounds?	/h/ /ā/
Say own: (own) Sounds?	/ō/ /n/	Say an: (an) Sounds?	/ă/ /n/
Say doe: (doe) Sounds?	/d/ /ō/	Say lie: (lie) Sounds?	/l/ /ī/

Day 12

High-Frequency Words

Now I'm going to show you how to read 4 more high-frequency words. Watch me, my turn.

(Display here.)
The word is here, as in the sentence "Here is my homework."
- **Watch me finger-stretch the sounds. /h/ /ē/ /r/** (Show thumb for /h/, pointer finger for /ē/, and middle finger for /r/.)
- **There are 3 sounds in the word *here*. This word is spelled with 4 letters, *h-e-r-e*.**

Now it's your turn. Word? here How many letters? 4
The letter names are h-e-r-e. Say them with me. h-e-r-e

(Use the process below to review the next 3 words.)

HFW List	
our /ou/ /r/	• **The word is ______. What is the word? ______** • **Listen for this word in the following sentence.** (Use the word in a sentence.) • **Watch me finger-stretch the sounds.** • **There are** (number) **sound(s) in the word ______.** • **This word is spelled with** (number) **letter(s), ______.** **Now it's your turn.** • **Word? ______ How many letter(s)? ______** • **The letter name(s) are ______. Say them with me. ______**
was /w/ /ə/ /z/	
when /hw/ /ĕ/ /n/	

our
was
when

Note: The vowel sound in the word *was* is a schwa sound /ə/. The vowel *a* makes the reduced short u sound.

FLUENCY: HIGH-FREQUENCY WORDS

Now we will practice reading the words we know.

(Display the high-frequency word grid. Prompt students by saying **"Word?"** at each box.)

when	here	was	our
no	so	his	that
find	play	go	yes
away	with	day	say

Reading

READ A STORY

Now, let's read a story.

Turn to page 19 in your workbook. Find the title of the story. Let's read it together. The Jet Set What do you think the story will be about? (Allow the students time to share their predictions.)

Now, find the first sentence of the story. Here are the steps:

1. Look at each word and decide if it's a high-frequency word.
   - If it's a high-frequency word, read the word.
   - If it's not a high-frequency word, point to the letters, say the sounds, and then read the word.
2. Use this routine to read all the sentences in the story.
3. After you read the story, we will read it together.

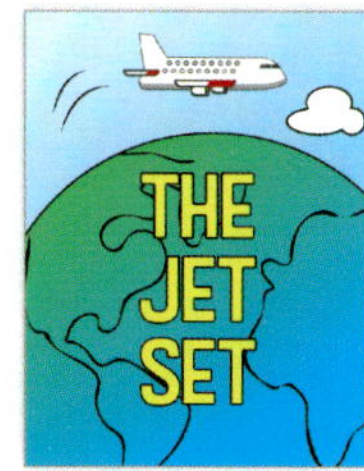

> **The Jet Set**
>
> The sun is up.
> Dad, Zac, and I have bags.
> "Can we go?" I say.
> With a nod, Dad says, "Yes."
> Do we hop in a cab? No.
> Do we get on a bus? No.
> Do we sit in a van? No.
> Dad, Zac, and I go up and up.
> We say, "Look at us."
> "We are the jet set."

(After students read, ask them what each person takes with them. **Each person takes bags.**)

Writing

WRITE SENTENCES

Now we'll practice writing sentences.

Answer with me as we do the first one together.

Let's write the following sentence: Here is Zig. Repeat it with me.
Here is Zig. (Hold up 1 finger for each word as you repeat the sentence.)

- **How many words do you hear? 3**
- **What is the first word? Here This is the high-frequency word spelled uppercase H, lowercase e-r-e.**
  - **Notice that H is uppercase because it's the first word in a sentence.**
- (Repeat the sentence.) **What is the second word? is This is the high-frequency word spelled i-s.**
- (Repeat the sentence.) **What is the last word? Zig This is a name, so the first letter is uppercase.**
  - **Say the sounds and letters. /z/ uppercase Z - /ĭ/ i - /g/ g**
- **Punctuation mark? period**
- **Read the sentence. Here is Zig.**

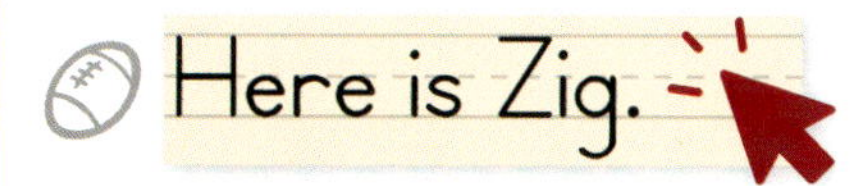

Day 12

Now it's your turn. Turn to page 23 in your Student Workbook. Find the line that has a football in front of it.

(Display word box.)

Above the line, there is a box that has some high-frequency words that we have learned. Let's read them together. **our, little, now, he**

our, little, now, he

Here are the steps:
1. I'll say the sentence and you repeat it.
2. I'll say each word, and before you write it, decide if it's a high-frequency word. Use the word boxes in your workbook to help you.
   - If it's a high-frequency word, write the letters.
   - If it's not a high-frequency word, break the word into sounds and write the letter for each sound.
3. Make sure the first letter in your sentence and all names are uppercase.
4. Put a punctuation mark at the end.
5. Then, read the sentence.

1. Zig is our pet rat.
2. Our rat is little.

Now that you have written 2 sentences, go back to the top and trace the first sentence. Finally, whisper read all 3 sentences.

Phonological Awareness Wrap-Up

PHONOLOGICAL AWARENESS: PHONEME SEGMENTATION

Today we are going to practice <u>segmenting sounds</u> in words with 2 sounds. Let's review the instructions:
- I'll say a word and you repeat it.
- Then, I'll tell you to segment, or say, all the sounds in the word. Ready?

Say buy: (buy) Sounds?	/b/ /ī/	Say us: (us) Sounds?	/ŭ/ /s/
Say am: (am) Sounds?	/ă/ /m/	Say zoo: (zoo) Sounds?	/z/ /ū/
Say if: (if) Sounds?	/ĭ/ /f/	Say guy: (guy) Sounds?	/g/ /ī/
Say shoe: (shoe) Sounds?	/sh/ /ū/	Say pay: (pay) Sounds?	/p/ /ā/
Say say: (say) Sounds?	/s/ /ā/	Say tea: (tea) Sounds?	/t/ /ē/
Say odd: (odd) Sounds?	/ŏ/ /d/	Say off: (off) Sounds?	/aw/ /f/
Say sigh: (sigh) Sounds?	/s/ /ī/	Say low: (low) Sounds?	/l/ /ō/
Say each: (each) Sounds?	/ē/ /ch/	Say is: (is) Sounds?	/ĭ/ /z/

DAY 13
Phonological Awareness Warm-Up

PHONOLOGICAL AWARENESS: PHONEME SEGMENTATION

Today we are going to practice <u>segmenting sounds</u> in words with 3 sounds.

Let's try one together.
- **Say <u>red</u>: (red) Finger-stretch and tell me the sounds in the word.**
/r/ /ĕ/ /d/

Now it's your turn. Here are the instructions:
- **I'll say a word and you repeat it.**
- **Then, I'll tell you to segment, or say, all the sounds in the word. Ready?**

Say kiss: (kiss) Sounds?	/k/ /ĭ/ /s/	**Say rag: (rag) Sounds?**	/r/ /ă/ /g/
Say pan: (pan) Sounds?	/p/ /ă/ /n/	**Say fun: (fun) Sounds?**	/f/ /ŭ/ /n/
Say dip: (dip) Sounds?	/d/ /ĭ/ /p/	**Say top: (top) Sounds?**	/t/ /ŏ/ /p/
Say back: (back) Sounds?	/b/ /ă/ /k/	**Say lip: (lip) Sounds?**	/l/ /ĭ/ /p/
Say shake: (shake) Sounds?	/sh/ /ā/ /k/	**Say bug: (bug) Sounds?**	/b/ /ŭ/ /g/
Say bike: (bike) Sounds?	/b/ /ī/ /k/	**Say pack: (pack) Sounds?**	/p/ /ă/ /k/
Say cat: (cat) Sounds?	/k/ /ă/ /t/	**Say sat: (sat) Sounds?**	/s/ /ă/ /t/
Say hot: (hot) Sounds?	/h/ /ŏ/ /t/	**Say pen: (pen) Sounds?**	/p/ /ĕ/ /n/

Letter-Sound Correspondence

WORD COMPLETION WITH PICTURES

Now we're going to fill in the missing sound in words. Look at each picture. Fill in the correct letter to complete the word. After you write the letter, whisper read the word.

I'll do the first one. This picture is <u>can</u>.
- **I finger-stretch can. /k/ /ă/ /n/**
- **I tap the letters and line while saying the sounds to see what sound is missing.** (Tap the letter *c*, the letter *a*, and the line.)
  - **The last sound /n/ is missing. The sound /n/ is spelled with the letter *n*.**
- **Next, I write the letter *n* in the space.**
- **Finally, I slide a finger under the word and whisper "can."**

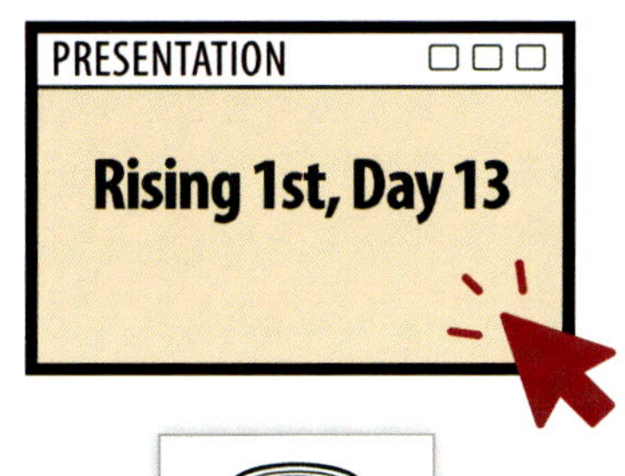

Day 13

Now it's your turn. Turn to page 23 in your Student Workbook. (Review the name of each picture with students before they begin.)

Here are the steps:
1. **Finger-stretch the sounds.**
2. **Tap the letters and line while saying the sounds.**
3. **Write the letter for the missing sound.**
4. **Whisper read the word.**

Answer Key

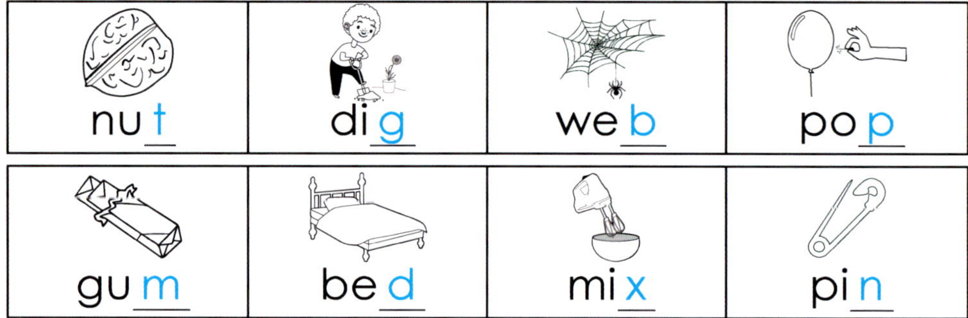

<table>
<tr><td>High-Frequency Words</td></tr>
</table>

High-Frequency Words

Now I'm going to show you how to read 4 more high-frequency words. Watch me, my turn.

(Display <u>eat</u>.)

eat

The word is eat, as in the sentence "We will eat pizza for dinner."
- **Watch me finger-stretch the sounds. /ē/ /t/** (Show thumb for /ē/ and pointer finger for /t/.)
- **There are 2 sounds in the word *eat*. This word is spelled with 3 letters, *e-a-t*.**

Now it's your turn. Word? eat How many letters? 3
The letter names are e-a-t. Say them with me. e-a-t

(Use the process below to review the next 3 words.)

saw
she
too

HFW List	
saw /s/ /aw/	• The word is _______. What is the word? _______ • Listen for this word in the following sentence. (Use the word in a sentence.) • Watch me finger-stretch the sounds. • There are <u>(number)</u> sound(s) in the word _______.
she /sh/ /ē/	• This word is spelled with <u>(number)</u> letter(s), _______. **Now it's your turn.**
too /t/ /ū/	• Word? _______ How many letter(s)? _______ • The letter name(s) are _______. Say them with me. _______

Note: Take a moment to compare the words *to* and *too*. Explain that the word *to* (t-o) means "towards or in a specific direction" (e.g., We go to school.). The word *too* (t-o-o) means "also or as well" and "more than enough or an excess" (e.g., I want some ice cream too. My feet are too big for the shoes.).

FLUENCY: HIGH-FREQUENCY WORDS

Now we will practice reading the words we know.

(Display the high-frequency word grid. Prompt students by saying **"Word?"** at each box.)

eat	she	saw	too
when	our	was	here
yes	no	so	go
with	his	that	away

Reading

READ SENTENCES

It's sentence time!

Turn to page 24 in your workbook. Find the line that has a lightbulb in front of it.

(Display word box.)
Above the line, there is a box with some high-frequency words that we have learned. Let's read them together. I, saw, eat, she, yes, now, have, too Now, put your pointer finger in front of the first word in the sentence.

I, saw, eat, she, yes, now, have, too

(Display sentence.)
Let's read the first sentence together. (Follow the same process from previous days. Read the bold high-frequency words and sound out the decodable words that are not bold.)

I saw Liz had a hot dog.

Now it's your turn. On the line that has a lightbulb in front of it, find the sentence that is next to the one we just read together. Put your pointer finger in front of the first word.

Let's review the steps:
1. **Look at each word and decide if it's a high-frequency word.**
   - **If the word is bold, it's a high-frequency word. Read the word.**
   - **If it's not a high-frequency word, point to the letters, say the sounds, and then read the word.**
2. **Continue until you read each word.**
3. **Then read the sentence.**

1. Can **I eat a** hot dog?
2. **She said yes**.
3. **Now I have a** hot dog **too**.

(After reading, point out that these 4 sentences tell a story. Ask students what Liz ate. **Liz ate a hot dog.**)

Day
13

Writing

WRITE SENTENCES

Now we'll practice writing sentences.

Answer with me as we do the first one together.

Let's write the following sentence: <u>Jax has jam.</u> Repeat it with me.
Jax has jam. (Hold up 1 finger for each word as you repeat the sentence.)
- **How many words do you hear? 3**
- **What is the first word? Jax**
  - **Sounds and letters? /j/ uppercase J - /ă/ a - /k/ /s/ x**
  - **Notice that J is uppercase because it's the first word in a sentence and is the first letter of a name.**
- (Repeat the sentence.) **What is the second word? has I write the high-frequency word spelled h-a-s.**
- (Repeat the sentence.) **What is the last word? jam**
  - **Sounds and letters? /j/ j - /ă/ a - /m/ m**
- **Punctuation mark? period**
- **Read the sentence. Jax has jam.**

 **Now it's your turn. Turn to page 24 in your Student Workbook. Find the line that has a lock in front of it.**

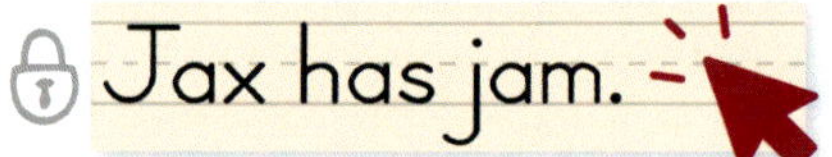

(Display word box.)
Above the line, there is a box that has some high-frequency words that we have learned. Let's read them together. has, too, eat, good

Here are the steps:
1. **I'll say the sentence and you repeat it.**
2. **After I say each word, decide if it's a high-frequency word. Use the word boxes in your workbook to help you.**
   - **If it's a high-frequency word, write the letters.**
   - **If it's not a high-frequency word, break the word into sounds and write the letter for each sound.**
3. **Make sure the first letter in your sentence and all names are uppercase.**
4. **Put a punctuation mark at the end.**
5. **Then, read the sentence.**

Now that you have written 3 sentences, go back to the top and trace the first sentence. Finally, whisper read all 4 sentences.

Phonological Awareness Wrap-Up

PHONOLOGICAL AWARENESS: PHONEME SEGMENTATION

Today we are going to practice <u>segmenting sounds</u> in words with 3 sounds. Let's review the instructions:
- I'll say a word and you repeat it.
- Then, I'll tell you to segment, or say, all the sounds in the word. Ready?

Say met: (met) Sounds?	/m/ /ĕ/ /t/	Say ripe: (ripe) Sounds?	/r/ /ī/ /p/
Say pick: (pick) Sounds?	/p/ /ĭ/ /k/	Say fat: (fat) Sounds?	/f/ /ă/ /t/
Say leg: (leg) Sounds?	/l/ /ĕ/ /g/	Say late: (late) Sounds?	/l/ /ā/ /t/
Say keep: (keep) Sounds?	/k/ /ē/ /p/	Say page: (page) Sounds?	/p/ /ā/ /j/
Say bad: (bad) Sounds?	/b/ /ă/ /d/	Say come: (come) Sounds?	/k/ /ŭ/ /m/
Say let: (let) Sounds?	/l/ /ĕ/ /t/	Say dog: (dog) Sounds?	/d/ /ŏ/ /g/
Say cape: (cape) Sounds?	/k/ /ā/ /p/	Say gum: (gum) Sounds?	/g/ /ŭ/ /m/
Say ship: (ship) Sounds?	/sh/ /ĭ/ /p/	Say cop: (cop) Sounds?	/k/ /ŏ/ /p/

DAY 14

Phonological Awareness Warm-Up

PHONOLOGICAL AWARENESS: PHONEME SEGMENTATION

Today we are going to practice <u>segmenting sounds</u> in words with 3 sounds. Let's review the instructions:
- I'll say a word and you repeat it.
- Then, I'll tell you to segment, or say, all the sounds in the word. Ready?

Say got: (got) Sounds?	/g/ /ŏ/ /t/	Say pet: (pet) Sounds?	/p/ /ĕ/ /t/
Say hill: (hill) Sounds?	/h/ /ĭ/ /l/	Say rose: (rose) Sounds?	/r/ /ō/ /z/
Say fan: (fan) Sounds?	/f/ /ă/ /n/	Say cheek: (cheek) Sounds?	/ch/ /ē/ /k/
Say nap: (nap) Sounds?	/n/ /ă/ /p/	Say mess: (mess) Sounds?	/m/ /ĕ/ /s/
Say lamb: (lamb) Sounds?	/l/ /ă/ /m/	Say head: (head) Sounds?	/h/ /ĕ/ /d/
Say bed: (bed) Sounds?	/b/ /ĕ/ /d/	Say mom: (mom) Sounds?	/m/ /ŏ/ /m/
Say goat: (goat) Sounds?	/g/ /ō/ /t/	Say beg: (beg) Sounds?	/b/ /ĕ/ /g/
Say miss: (miss) Sounds?	/m/ /ĭ/ /s/	Say hat: (hat) Sounds?	/h/ /ă/ /t/

Day 14

High-Frequency Words

Now I'm going to show you how to read 4 more high-frequency words. Watch me, my turn.

(Display <u>as</u>.)
The word is <u>as</u>, as in the sentence "The dog is as big as a pony."
- **Watch me finger-stretch the sounds. /ă/ /z/** (Show thumb for /ă/ and pointer finger for /z/.)
- **There are 2 sounds in the word *as*. This word is spelled with 2 letters, *a-s*.**

Now it's your turn. Word? as How many letters? 2
The letter names are a-s. Say them with me. a-s

(Use the process below to review the next 3 words.)

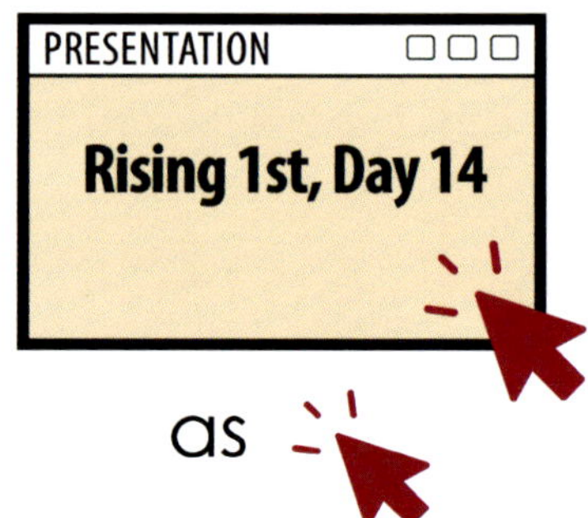

HFW List	
into /ĭ/ /n/ /t/ /ū/	• **The word is ______. What is the word? ______** • **Listen for this word in the following sentence.** (Use the word in a sentence.) • **Watch me finger-stretch the sounds.** • **There are** ^(number) **sound(s) in the word ______.** • **This word is spelled with** ^(number) **letter(s), ______.**
of /ŭ/ /v/	**Now it's your turn.** • **Word? ______ How many letter(s)? ______** • **The letter name(s) are ______. Say them with me. ______**
there /<u>th</u>/ /air/	

FLUENCY: HIGH-FREQUENCY WORDS

Now we will practice reading the words we know.

(Display the high-frequency word grid. Prompt students by saying **"Word?"** at each box.)

as	into	there	of
she	was	so	eat
here	go	too	when
yes	saw	our	no

cat

Reading

READ A STORY

Now we will reread the story, *The Jet Set*.

 **Turn to page 19 in your workbook. Find the title of the story. Let's read it together. The Jet Set**

Now, find the first sentence of the story. Here are the steps:
1. **Look at each word and decide if it's a high-frequency word.**
    -   **If it's a high-frequency word, read the word.**
    -   **If it's not a high-frequency word, point to the letters, say the sounds, and then read the word.**
2. **Use this routine to read all the sentences in the story.**

We'll discuss the story when you've finished reading.

> **The Jet Set**
>
> The sun is up.
> Dad, Zac, and I have bags.
> "Can we go?" I say.
> With a nod, Dad says, "Yes."
> Do we hop in a cab? No.
> Do we get on a bus? No.
> Do we sit in a van? No.
> Dad, Zac, and I go up and up.
> We say, "Look at us."
> "We are the jet set."

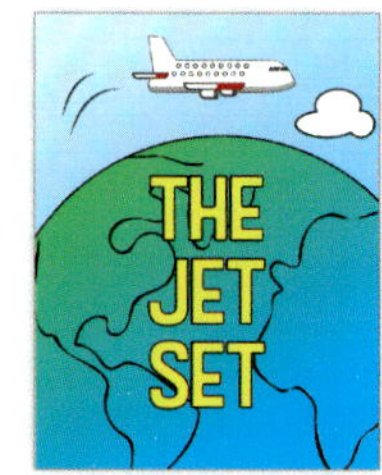

(After reading, ask students how the family travels. **They travel in a jet.**)

 **Teacher Tip**

If there is time after reading and discussing the story, you can ask students to draw a picture about the story and share it with another student. If you are teaching remotely on a videoconferencing platform, ask students to hold their drawings up to the camera to share them.

Writing

WRITE SENTENCES

Now we'll practice writing sentences.

Answer with me as we do the first one together.

Let's write the following sentence: There was a pig. Repeat it with me. There was a pig. (Hold up 1 finger for each word as you repeat the sentence.)

- **How many words do you hear? 4**
- **What is the first word? There I write the high-frequency word spelled uppercase T, lowercase h-e-r-e.**
  - **Notice that T is uppercase because it's the first word in a sentence.**
- (Repeat the sentence.) **What is the second word? was I write the high-frequency word spelled w-a-s.**
- (Repeat the sentence.) **What is the third word? a I write the high-frequency word spelled a.**
- (Repeat the sentence.) **What is the last word? pig**
  - **Sounds and letters? /p/ p - /ĭ/ i - /g/ g**
- **Punctuation mark? period**
- **Read the sentence. There was a pig.**

 **Now it's your turn. Turn to page 25 in your Student Workbook. Find the line that has a bike in front of it.**

(Display word box.)
Above the line, there is a box that has some high-frequency words that we have learned. Let's read them together. he, was, with, of

Here are the steps:
1. **I'll say the sentence and you repeat it.**
2. **After I say each word, decide if it's a high-frequency word. Use the word boxes in your workbook to help you.**
   - **If it's a high-frequency word, write the letters.**
   - **If it's not a high-frequency word, break the word into sounds and write the letter for each sound.**
3. **Make sure the first letter in your sentence and all names are uppercase.**
4. **Put a punctuation mark at the end.**
5. **Then, read the sentence.**

Now that you have written 2 sentences, go back to the top and trace the first sentence. Finally, whisper read all 3 sentences.

There was a pig.

he, was, with, of

1. He was a pig with a wig.
2. It was a wig of a yak.

Phonological Awareness Wrap-Up

PHONOLOGICAL AWARENESS: PHONEME SEGMENTATION

Today we are going to practice <u>segmenting sounds</u> in words with 3 sounds. Let's review the instructions:
- I'll say a word and you repeat it.
- Then, I'll tell you to segment, or say, all the sounds in the word. Ready?

Say seat: (seat) Sounds?	/s/ /ē/ /t/	Say pat: (pat) Sounds?	/p/ /ă/ /t/
Say kite: (kite) Sounds?	/k/ /ī/ /t/	Say man: (man) Sounds?	/m/ /ă/ /n/
Say coat: (coat) Sounds?	/k/ /ō/ /t/	Say nose: (nose) Sounds?	/n/ /ō/ /z/
Say lap: (lap) Sounds?	/l/ /ă/ /p/	Say fin: (fin) Sounds?	/f/ /ĭ/ /n/
Say run: (run) Sounds?	/r/ /ŭ/ /n/	Say rag: (rag) Sounds?	/r/ /ă/ /g/
Say set: (set) Sounds?	/s/ /ĕ/ /t/	Say mop: (mop) Sounds?	/m/ /ŏ/ /p/
Say mutt: (mutt) Sounds?	/m/ /ŭ/ /t/	Say kid: (kid) Sounds?	/k/ /ĭ/ /d/
Say big: (big) Sounds?	/b/ /ĭ/ /g/	Say chin: (chin) Sounds?	/ch/ /ĭ/ /n/

DAY 15

Phonological Awareness Warm-Up

PHONOLOGICAL AWARENESS: PHONEME SEGMENTATION

Today we are going to practice <u>segmenting sounds</u> in words with 2 or 3 sounds. Let's review the instructions:
- I'll say a word and you repeat it.
- Then, I'll tell you to segment, or say, all the sounds in the word. Ready?

Say chat: (chat) Sounds?	/ch/ /ă/ /t/	Say shy: (shy) Sounds?	/sh/ /ī/
Say nut: (nut) Sounds?	/n/ /ŭ/ /t/	Say did: (did) Sounds?	/d/ /ĭ/ /d/
Say sheep: (sheep) Sounds?	/sh/ /ē/ /p/	Say net: (net) Sounds?	/n/ /ĕ/ /t/
Say date: (date) Sounds?	/d/ /ā/ /t/	Say you: (you) Sounds?	/y/ /ū/
Say wet: (wet) Sounds?	/w/ /ĕ/ /t/	Say push: (push) Sounds?	/p/ /oo/ /sh/
Say mow: (mow) Sounds?	/m/ /ō/	Say itch: (itch) Sounds?	/ĭ/ /ch/
Say hum: (hum) Sounds?	/h/ /ŭ/ /m/	Say knock: (knock) Sounds?	/n/ /ŏ/ /k/
Say bone: (bone) Sounds?	/b/ /ō/ /n/	Say sew: (sew) Sounds?	/s/ /ō/

Letter-Sound Correspondence

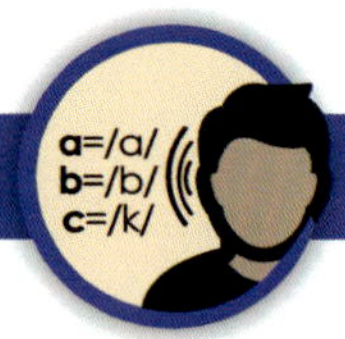

WORD COMPLETION WITH PICTURES

Now we're going to fill in the missing sound in words. Look at each picture. Fill in the correct letter to complete the word. After you write the letter, whisper read the word.

I'll do the first one. This picture is <u>sit</u>.
- I finger-stretch sit. /s/ /ĭ/ /t/
- I tap the letters and line while saying the sounds to see which sound is missing. (Tap the letter *s*, the letter *i*, and the line.)
  - The last sound /t/ is missing. The sound /t/ is spelled with the letter *t*.
- Next, I write the letter *t* in the space.
- Finally, I slide a finger under the word and whisper "sit."

Now it's your turn. Turn to page 25 in your Student Workbook. (Review the name of each picture with students before they begin.)

Here are the steps:
1. Finger-stretch the sounds.
2. Tap the letters and line while saying the sounds.
3. Write the letter for the missing sound.
4. Whisper read the word.

Answer Key

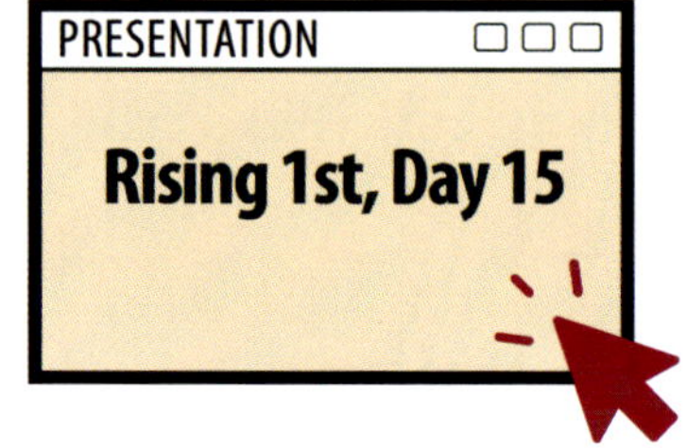

High-Frequency Words

Now I'm going to show you how to read 4 more high-frequency words. Watch me, my turn.

(Display <u>one</u>.)
The word is <u>one</u>, as in the sentence "We have one cat."
- **Watch me finger-stretch the sounds. /w/ /ŭ/ /n/** (Show thumb for /w/, pointer finger for /ŭ/, and middle finger for /n/.)
- **There are 3 sounds in the word** *one*. **This word is spelled with three letters,** *o-n-e.*

Now it's your turn. Word? one How many letters? 3
The letter names are o-n-e. Say them with me. o-n-e

(Use the process below to review the next 3 words.)

one

HFW List	
two /t/ /ū/	• **The word is _______. What is the word? ______** • **Listen for this word in the following sentence.** (Use the word in a sentence.) • **Watch me finger-stretch the sounds.** • **There are** (number) **sound(s) in the word ______.** • **This word is spelled with** (number) **letter(s), ______.** **Now it's your turn.** • **Word? ______ How many letter(s)? ______** • **The letter name(s) are ______. Say them with me. ______**
three /th/ /r/ /ē/	
four /f/ /or/	

two
three
four

FLUENCY: HIGH-FREQUENCY WORDS

Now we will practice reading the words we know.

(Display the high-frequency word grid. Prompt students by saying **"Word?"** at each box.)

three	one	four	two
as	into	of	there
eat	saw	she	too
here	our	was	when

Day 15

Reading

READ SENTENCES

It's sentence time!

 **Turn to page 26 in your workbook. Find the line that has a ship in front of it.**

(Display word box.)
Above the line, there is a box with some high-frequency words that we have learned. Let's read them together. one, two, three, what, four
Now, put your pointer finger in front of the first word in the sentence.

one, two, three, what, four

(Display sentence.)
Let's read the first sentence together. (Follow the same process from previous days. Read the bold high-frequency words and sound out the decodable words that are not bold.)

One and one is two.

Now it's your turn. On the line that has a ship in front of it, find the sentence that is next to the one we just read together. Put your pointer finger in front of the first word.

Let's review the steps:
1. **Look at each word.**
   – **All the words in the next 3 sentences are bold high-frequency words. Read each word without sounding it out.**
2. **Continue until you read each word.**
3. **Then read the sentence.**

(After reading, point out that these 4 sentences tell a story. Ask students what two and one is. **three**)

1. **Two and one is three**.
2. **What is three and one**?
3. **Three and one is four**.

Writing

WRITE SENTENCES

Now we'll practice writing sentences.

Answer with me as we do the first one together.

Let's write the following sentence: One red hen.
Repeat it with me. One red hen. (Hold up 1 finger for each word as you repeat the sentence.)
- **How many words do you hear? 3**
- **What is the first word? One I write the high-frequency word spelled uppercase O, lowercase n-e.**
  – **Notice that O is uppercase because it's the first word in a sentence.**
- (Repeat the sentence.) **What is the second word? red**
  – **Sounds and letters? /r/ r - /ĕ/ e - /d/ d**

- (Repeat the sentence.) **What is the last word? hen**
  - **Sounds and letters? /h/ h - /ĕ/ e- /n/ n**
- **Punctuation mark? period**
- **Read the sentence. One red hen.**

Now it's your turn. Turn to page 26 in your Student Workbook. Find the line that has a pencil in front of it.

(Display word box.)

Above the line, there is a box that has some high-frequency words that we have learned. Let's read them together. two, three, little, four

two, three, little, four

Let's review the steps:

1. **I'll say the sentence and you repeat it.**
2. **After I say each word, decide if it's a high-frequency word. Use the word boxes in your workbook to help you.**
   - **If it's a high-frequency word, write the letters.**
   - **If it's not a high-frequency word, break the word into sounds and write the letter for each sound.**
3. **Make sure the first letter in your sentence and all names are uppercase.**
4. **Put a punctuation mark at the end.**
5. **Then, read the sentence.**

1. Two big rams.
2. Three little pups.
3. Four fat cod.

Now that you have written 3 sentences, go back to the top and trace the first sentence. Finally, whisper read all 4 sentences.

Phonological Awareness Wrap-Up

PHONOLOGICAL AWARENESS: PHONEME SEGMENTATION

Today we are going to practice <u>segmenting sounds</u> in words with 2 or 3 sounds. Let's review the instructions:

- **I'll say a word and you repeat it.**
- **Then, I'll tell you to segment, or say, all the sounds in the word. Ready?**

Say if: (if) Sounds?	**/ĭ/ /f/**	**Say why: (why) Sounds?**	**/hw/ /ī/**
Say cool: (cool) Sounds?	**/k/ /ū/ /l/**	**Say side: (side) Sounds?**	**/s/ /ī/ /d/**
Say an: (an) Sounds?	**/ă/ /n/**	**Say neck: (neck) Sounds?**	**/n/ /ĕ/ /k/**
Say dot: (dot) Sounds?	**/d/ /ŏ/ /t/**	**Say gate: (gate) Sounds?**	**/g/ /ā/ /t/**
Say what: (what) Sounds?	**/hw/ /ŭ/ /t/**	**Say new: (new) Sounds?**	**/n/ /ū/**
Say say: (say) Sounds?	**/s/ /ā/**	**Say day: (day) Sounds?**	**/d/ /ā/**
Say rake: (rake) Sounds?	**/r/ /ā/ /k/**	**Say when: (when) Sounds?**	**/hw/ /ĕ/ /n/**
Say cub: (cub) Sounds?	**/k/ /ŭ/ /b/**	**Say feet: (feet) Sounds?**	**/f/ /ē/ /t/**

Day 16

Days 16–20: Short Vowels, Reading, & Writing 3

Learning Objective

Students demonstrate understanding of how to read sentences and short stories with decodable VC and CVC words and selected irregularly spelled high-frequency words. Additionally, they write short sentences composed of these types of words.

DAY 16

Phonological Awareness Warm-Up

PHONOLOGICAL AWARENESS: BLENDING 2 AND 3 PHONEMES

Today we are going to practice <u>blending 2 or 3 sounds</u> to make words.

Let's practice together.
- I'll say the sounds. /s/ /ō/
  – Now, you blend them. Word? so
- Here's the next one. /m/ /ē/
  – Word? me

Now it's your turn. Here are the instructions:
- I'll say the sounds.
- Then, I'll ask you to say the word. Ready?

/l/ /ĭ/ /p/: Word?	lip	/d/ /ŭ/ /k/: Word?	duck
/ē/ /ch/: Word?	each	/k/ /yū/ /b/: Word?	cube
/g/ /ĕ/ /t/: Word?	get	/b/ /ar/ /k/: Word?	bark
/ŏ/ /d/: Word?	odd	/s/ /ĭ/ /p/: Word?	sip
/h/ /ŏ/ /p/: Word?	hop	/r/ /ā/ /n/: Word?	rain
/m/ /ŭ/ /ch/: Word?	much	/b/ /ē/ /k/: Word?	beak
/s/ /ă/ /d/: Word?	sad	/k/ /ē/: Word?	key
/l/ /ī/ /f/: Word?	life	/j/ /ĕ/ /t/: Word?	jet

Letter-Sound Correspondence

WORD COMPLETION WITH PICTURES

Now we're going to fill in the missing sound in words. Look at each picture. Fill in the correct letter to complete the word. After you write the letter, whisper read the word.

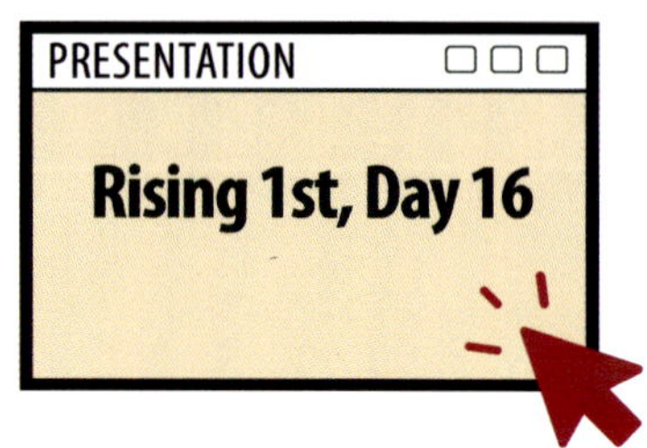

I'll do the first one. This picture is <u>gum</u>.

- I finger-stretch gum. /g/ /ŭ/ /m/
- I tap the letters and line while saying the sounds to see what sound is missing. (Tap the letter *g*, the line, and the letter *m*.)
  - The middle sound /ŭ/ is missing. The sound /ŭ/ is spelled with the letter *u*.
- Next, I write the letter *u* in the space.
- Finally, I slide a finger under the word and whisper "gum."

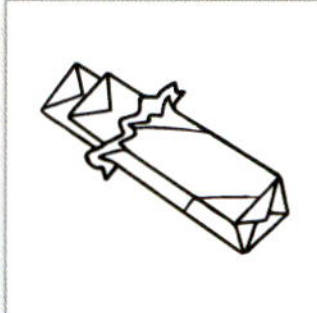

 Now it's your turn. Turn to page 29 in your Student Workbook. (Review the name of each picture with students before they begin.)

Here are the steps:
1. Finger-stretch the sounds.
2. Tap the letters and line while saying the sounds.
3. Write the letter for the missing sound.
4. Whisper read the word.

Answer Key

High-Frequency Words

Now I'm going to show you how to read 4 more high-frequency words. Watch me, my turn.

(Display <u>all</u>.)

The word is <u>all</u>, as in the sentence "She has all the crayons."
- Watch me finger-stretch the sounds. /aw/ /l/ (Show thumb for /aw/ and pointer finger for /l/.)
- There are 2 sounds in the word *all*. This word is spelled with 3 letters, *a-l-l*.

Now it's your turn. Word? all How many letters? 3
The letter names are a-l-l. Say them with me. a-l-l

(Use the process below to review the next 3 words.)

HFW List	
out /ou/ /t/	• **The word is ______. What is the word? ______** • **Listen for this word in the following sentence.** (Use the word in a sentence.) • **Watch me finger-stretch the sounds.** • **There are** (number) **sound(s) in the word ______.** • **This word is spelled with** (number) **letter(s), ______.** **Now it's your turn.** • **Word? ______ How many letter(s)? ______** • **The letter name(s) are ______. Say them with me. ______**
well /w/ /ĕ/ /l/	
will /w/ /ĭ/ /l/	

FLUENCY: HIGH-FREQUENCY WORDS

Now we will practice reading the words we know.

(Display the high-frequency word grid. Prompt students by saying **"Word?"** at each box.)

out	all	will	well
three	of	she	eat
as	one	four	there
too	two	into	saw

Reading

READ SENTENCES

It's sentence time!

 **Turn to page 30 in your workbook, find the line that has a canoe in front of it.**

(Display word box.)
Above the line, there is a box with some high-frequency words that we have learned. Let's read them together. **all, four, play, well, what, will**
Now, put your pointer finger in front of the first word in the sentence.

all, four, play, well, what, will

(Display sentence.)
Let's read the first sentence together. (Follow the same process from previous days. Read the bold high-frequency words and sound out the decodable words that are not bold.)

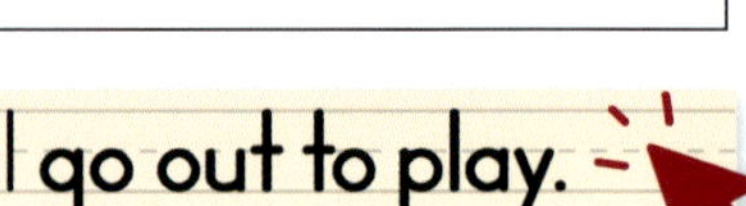

Now it's your turn. On the line that has a canoe in front of it, find the sentence that is next to the one we just read together. Put your pointer finger in front of the first word.

Let's review the steps:
1. **Look at each word and decide if it's a high-frequency word.**
   - **If the word is bold, it's a high-frequency word. Read the word.**
   - **If it's not a high-frequency word, point to the letters, say the sounds, and then read the word.**
2. **Continue until you read each word.**
3. **Then read the sentence.**

(After reading, ask the students who Wes and Val play with. **Wes and Val play with Rex and Pam.**)

> 1. **They see** Rex **and** Pam.
> 2. **All four play well.**
> 3. **What will they do**?

Writing

WRITE SENTENCES

Now we'll practice writing sentences.

Answer with me as we do the first one together.

Let's write the following sentence: Can you fix the tap?
Repeat it. Can you fix the tap? (Hold up 1 finger for each word as you repeat the sentence.)
- **How many words do you hear? 5**
- **What is the first word? Can**
  - **Sounds and letters? /k/ uppercase C - /ă/ a - /n/ n**
  - **Notice that C is uppercase because it's the first word in a sentence.**
- (Repeat the sentence.) **What is the second word? you I write the high-frequency word spelled y-o-u.**
- (Repeat the sentence.) **What is the third word? fix**
  - **Sounds and letters? /f/ f - /ĭ/ i - /k/ /s/ x**
- (Repeat the sentence.) **What is the fourth word? the I write the high-frequency word spelled t-h-e.**
- (Repeat the sentence.) **What is the last word? tap**
  - **Sounds and letters? /t/ t - /ă/ a - /p/ p**
- **Punctuation mark? question mark**
- **Read the sentence. Can you fix the tap?**

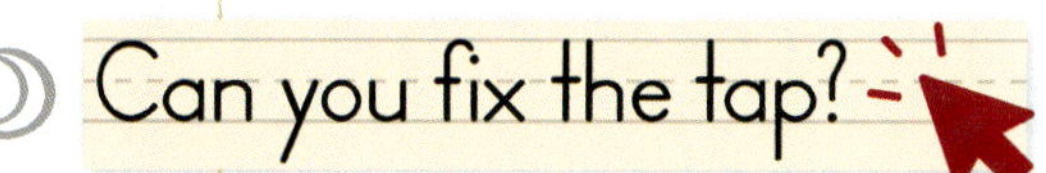

Now it's your turn. Turn to page 30 in your Student Workbook. Find the line that has a moon in front of it.

(Display word box.)

Above the line, there is a box that has some high-frequency words that we have learned. Let's read them together. **I, have, will, well, yes, good, go**

I, have, will, well, yes, good, go

Here are the steps:

1. I'll say the sentence and you repeat it.
2. I'll say each word, and before you write it, decide if it's a high-frequency word. Use the word boxes in your workbook to help you.
   – If it's a high-frequency word, write the letters.
   – If it's not a high-frequency word, break the word into sounds and write the letter for each sound.
3. Make sure the first letter in your sentence and all names are uppercase.
4. Put a punctuation mark at the end.
5. Then, read the sentence.

Note: The word *yes* is decodable but it's in the word box because /y/ at the beginning of a word can be difficult.

1. I have a kit to fix it.
2. Will you fix it well?
3. Yes, it is good to go.

Now that you have written 3 sentences, go back to the top and trace the first sentence. Finally, whisper read all 4 sentences.

Phonological Awareness Wrap-Up

PHONOLOGICAL AWARENESS: BLENDING 2 AND 3 PHONEMES

Now, we are going to practice <u>blending 2 or 3 sounds</u> to make words.

Let's practice one together.
- /sh/ /ē/: Word? **she**

Now it's your turn. Let's review the instructions:
- I'll say the sounds.
- Then, I'll ask you to say the word. Ready?

/ŭ/ /p/: Word?	**up**	/r/ /ō/ /p/: Word?	**rope**
/k/ /ē/ /p/: Word?	**keep**	/y/ /or/: Word?	**your**
/ă/ /m/: Word?	**am**	/f/ /ŭ/ /n/: Word?	**fun**
/h/ /ă/ /d/: Word?	**had**	/p/ /ō/ /k/: Word?	**poke**
/s/ /ŏ/ /b/: Word?	**sob**	/sh/ /ā/ /p/: Word?	**shape**
/m/ /ar/ /k/: Word?	**mark**	/p/ /ē/ /z/: Word?	**peas**
/z/ /ă/ /p/: Word?	**zap**	/f/ /ar/ /m/: Word?	**farm**
/m/ /ū/ /n/: Word?	**moon**	/w/ /ĭ/ /sh/: Word?	**wish**

DAY 17

Phonological Awareness Warm-Up

PHONOLOGICAL AWARENESS: ISOLATE INITIAL AND FINAL PHONEMES

Today we're going to practice saying the <u>first or last sound</u> in a word.

Let's practice together. I'll answer with you.
- Say <u>me</u>: (**me**) Last sound? **/ē/**
- Say <u>go</u>: (**go**) First sound? **/g/**

Now it's your turn. Here are the instructions:
- I'll say a word and you repeat it.
- Then, I'll ask you to tell me the first or last sound. Ready?

Say fill: (**fill**) First sound?	**/f/**	Say shy: (**shy**) Last sound?	**/ī/**
Say he: (**he**) First sound?	**/h/**	Say if: (**if**) Last sound?	**/f/**
Say chin: (**chin**) First sound?	**/ch/**	Say big: (**big**) Last sound?	**/g/**
Say ham: (**ham**) First sound?	**/h/**	Say dish: (**dish**) Last sound?	**/sh/**
Say light: (**light**) First sound?	**/l/**	Say his: (**his**) Last sound?	**/z/**
Say toe: (**toe**) First sound?	**/t/**	Say she: (**she**) Last sound?	**/ē/**
Say miss: (**miss**) First sound?	**/m/**	Say laugh: (**laugh**) Last sound?	**/f/**
Say bad: (**bad**) First sound?	**/b/**	Say show: (**show**) Last sound?	**/ō/**

High-Frequency Words

Now I'm going to show you how to read 4 more high-frequency words. Watch me, my turn.

(Display <u>help</u>.)
The word is <u>help</u>, as in the sentence "I can help you study."
- **Watch me finger-stretch the sounds. /h/ /ĕ/ /l/ /p/** (Show thumb for /h/, pointer finger for /ĕ/, middle finger for /l/, and ring finger for /p/.)
- **There are 4 sounds in the word *help*. This word is spelled with 4 letters, *h-e-l-p*.**

Now it's your turn. Word? help How many letters? 4
The letter names are h-e-l-p. Say them with me. h-e-l-p

(Use the process below to review the next 3 words.)

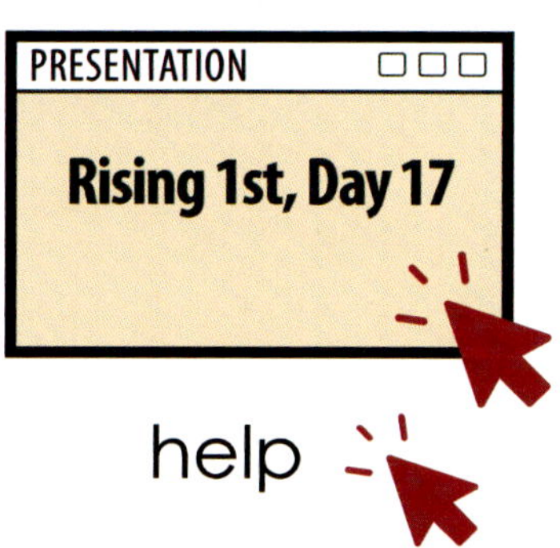

HFW List	
new /n/ /ū/	• **The word is ______. What is the word?** ______ • **Listen for this word in the following sentence.** (Use the word in a sentence.) • **Watch me finger-stretch the sounds.** • **There are** (number) **sound(s) in the word** ______. • **This word is spelled with** (number) **letter(s),** ______.
under /ŭ/ /n/ /d/ /er/	**Now it's your turn.** • **Word?** ______ **How many letter(s)?** ______
went /w/ /ĕ/ /n/ /t/	• **The letter name(s) are** ______. **Say them with me.** ______

FLUENCY: HIGH-FREQUENCY WORDS

Now we will practice reading the words we know.

(Display the high-frequency word grid. Prompt students by saying **"Word?"** at each box.)

help	under	went	new
out	all	four	one
as	into	well	three
of	will	two	there

Reading

READ A STORY

Now, let's read a story.

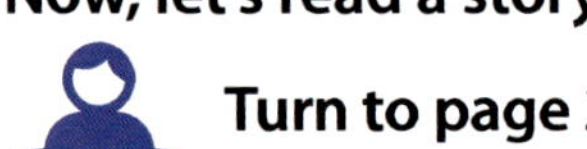 **Turn to page 27 in your workbook. Find the title of the story. Let's read the title together and then you'll tell me what you think the story will be about.** (Allow the students time to share their predictions.)

1. **Look at each word and decide if it's a high-frequency word.**
   - **If it's a high-frequency word, read the word.**
   - **If it's not a high-frequency word, point to the letters, say the sounds, and then read the word.**
2. **Use this routine to read all the sentences in the story.**
3. **After you read the story, we will read it together.**

> **As Good as New**
> I am Rex and I have a hat.
> I hop and bop with my hat.
> I rap and tap with my hat.
> But now it has a rip.
> Kim said, "Get rid of it."
> I went to Yun.
> He said, "Let me see."
> In a bit, I got my hat.
> "Have a look," said Yun.
> I said, "It is as good as new."

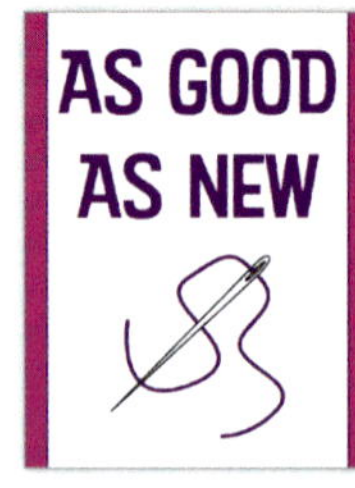

(After reading, ask students what is wrong with Rex's hat. **It has a rip.**)

Writing

WRITE SENTENCES

Now we'll practice writing sentences.

Answer with me as we do the first one together.

Let's write the following sentence: Nan is the new kid.
Repeat it. Nan is the new kid. (Hold up 1 finger for each word as you repeat the sentence.)
- **How many words do you hear? 5**
- **What is the first word? Nan**
  - **Sounds and letters? /n/ uppercase N - /ă/ a - /n/ n**
- (Repeat the sentence.) **What is the second word? is** I write the high-frequency word spelled i-s.
- (Repeat the sentence.) **What is the third word? the** I write the high-frequency word spelled t-h-e.
- (Repeat the sentence.) **What is the fourth word? new** I write the high-frequency word spelled n-e-w.
- (Repeat the sentence.) **What is the last word? kid**
  - **Sounds and letters? /k/ k - /ĭ/ i - /d/ d**
- **Punctuation mark? period**
- **Read the sentence. Nan is the new kid.**

 **Now it's your turn. Turn to page 31 in your Student Workbook. Find the line that has a lightning bolt in front of it.**

(Display word box.)
Above the line, there is a box that has some high-frequency words that we have learned. Let's read them together. she, help, went, under

Here are the steps:
1. **I'll say the sentence and you repeat it.**
2. **I'll say each word, and before you write it, decide if it's a high-frequency word. Use the word boxes in your workbook to help you.**
   - **If it's a high-frequency word, write the letters.**
   - **If it's not a high-frequency word, break the word into sounds and write the letter for each sound.**
3. **Make sure the first letter in your sentence and all names are uppercase.**
4. **Put a punctuation mark at the end.**
5. **Then, read the sentence.**

Now that you have written 3 sentences, go back to the top and trace the first sentence. Finally, whisper read all 4 sentences.

she, help, went, under

1. She can help us win.
2. Nan went under the net.
3. She hops up for the tip.

Day 17

Phonological Awareness Wrap-Up

PHONOLOGICAL AWARENESS: ISOLATE INITIAL AND FINAL PHONEMES

Now we're going to practice saying the <u>first or last sound</u> in a word.

Let's review the instructions:
- I'll say a word and you repeat it.
- Then, I'll ask you to tell me the first or last sound. Ready?

Say boo: (boo) First sound?	/b/	Say park: (park) Last sound?	/k/
Say pay: (pay) First sound?	/p/	Say in: (in) Last sound?	/n/
Say sore: (sore) First sound?	/s/	Say bag: (bag) Last sound?	/g/
Say chop: (chop) First sound?	/ch/	Say pine: (pine) Last sound?	/n/
Say oat: (oat) First sound?	/ō/	Say fizz: (fizz) Last sound?	/z/
Say right: (right) First sound?	/r/	Say cab: (cab) Last sound?	/b/
Say way: (way) First sound?	/w/	Say wall: (wall) Last sound?	/l/
Say look: (look) First sound?	/l/	Say tough: (tough) Last sound?	/f/

DAY 18

Phonological Awareness Warm-Up

PHONOLOGICAL AWARENESS: PHONEME SEGMENTATION

Today we are going to practice <u>segmenting phonemes</u> in words.

Let's try one together.
- Say no: (no) Sounds? /n/ /ō/

Now it's your turn. Here are the instructions:
- I'll say a word and you repeat it.
- Then, I'll ask you to tell me the sounds in the word. Ready?

Say as: (as) Sounds?	/ă/ /z/	Say show: (show) Sounds?	/sh/ /ō/
Say toe: (toe) Sounds?	/t/ /ō/	Say way: (way) Sounds?	/w/ /ā/
Say in: (in) Sounds?	/ĭ/ /n/	Say she: (she) Sounds?	/sh/ /ē/
Say odd: (odd) Sounds?	/ŏ/ /d/	Say knee: (knee) Sounds?	/n/ /ē/
Say sigh: (sigh) Sounds?	/s/ /ī/	Say low: (low) Sounds?	/l/ /ō/
Say at: (at) Sounds?	/ă/ /t/	Say is: (is) Sounds?	/ĭ/ /z/
Say up: (up) Sounds?	/ŭ/ /p/	Say ate: (ate) Sounds?	/ā/ /t/
Say ice: (ice) Sounds?	/ī/ /s/	Say pie: (pie) Sounds?	/p/ /ī/

Letter-Sound Correspondence

WORD COMPLETION WITH PICTURES

Now we're going to fill in the missing sound in words. Look at each picture. Fill in the correct letter to complete the word. After you write the letter, whisper read the word.

I'll do the first one. This picture is fox.
- I finger-stretch fox. /f/ /ŏ/ /k/ /s/
- I tap the letters and line while saying the sounds to see what sound is missing. (Tap the letter *f*, the line, and the letter *x*.)
  - The middle sound /ŏ/ is missing. The sound /ŏ/ is spelled with the letter *o*.
- Next, I write the letter *o* in the space.
- Finally, I slide a finger under the word and whisper "fox."

Now it's your turn. Turn to page 31 in your Student Workbook. (Review the name of each picture with students before they begin.)

Here are the steps:
1. Finger-stretch the sounds.
2. Tap the letters and line while saying the sounds.
3. Write the letter for the missing sound.
4. Whisper read the word.

Answer Key

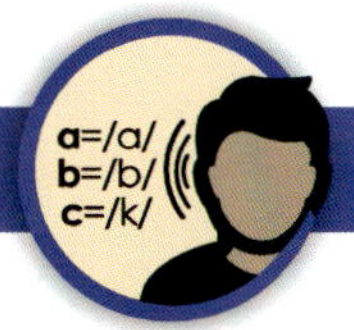

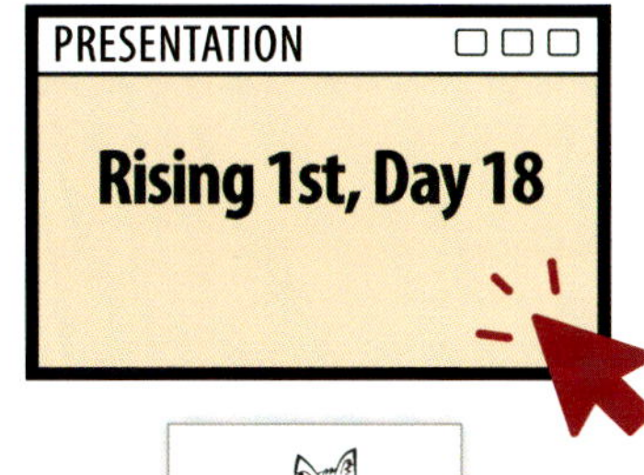

High-Frequency Words

Now I'm going to show you how to read 4 more high-frequency words. Watch me, my turn.

(Display must.)
The word is <u>must</u>, as in the sentence "You must go to bed early."
- **Watch me finger-stretch the sounds. /m/ /ŭ/ /s/ /t/** (Show thumb for /m/, pointer finger for /ŭ/, middle finger for /s/, and ring finger for /t/.)
- **There are 4 sounds in the word *must*. This word is spelled with 4 letters, *m-u-s-t*.**

Day 18

Now it's your turn. Word? must How many letters? 4
The letter names are m-u-s-t. Say them with me. m-u-s-t

(Use the process below to review the next 3 words.)

HFW List
please /p/ /l/ /ē/ /z/
soon /s/ /ū/ /n/
where /hw/ /air/

- **The word is _______. What is the word? _______**
- **Listen for this word in the following sentence.** (Use the word in a sentence.)
- **Watch me finger-stretch the sounds.**
- **There are** (number) **sound(s) in the word _______.**
- **This word is spelled with** (number) **letter(s), _______.**

Now it's your turn.
- **Word? _______ How many letter(s)? _______**
- **The letter name(s) are _______. Say them with me. _______**

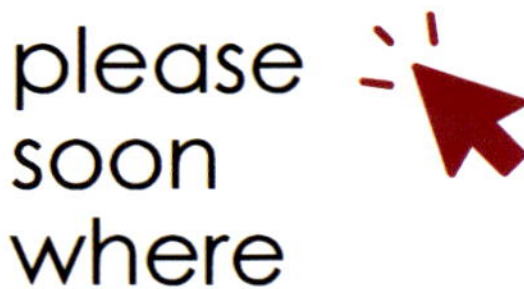

FLUENCY: HIGH-FREQUENCY WORDS

Now we will practice reading the words we know.

(Display the high-frequency word grid. Prompt students by saying **"Word?"** at each box.)

soon	must	where	please
new	went	under	help
out	will	well	all
two	four	three	one

Reading

READ SENTENCES

It's sentence time!

Turn to page 32 in your workbook. Find the line that has a puppy in front of it.

(Display word box.)
Above the line, there is a box with some high-frequency words that we have learned. Let's read them together. will, soon, I, must, find, my, please, where, go Now, put your pointer finger in front of the first word in the sentence.

will, soon, I, must, find, my, please, where, go

(Display sentence.)
Let's read the first sentence together. (Follow the same process from previous days. Read the bold high-frequency words and sound out the decodable words that are not bold.)

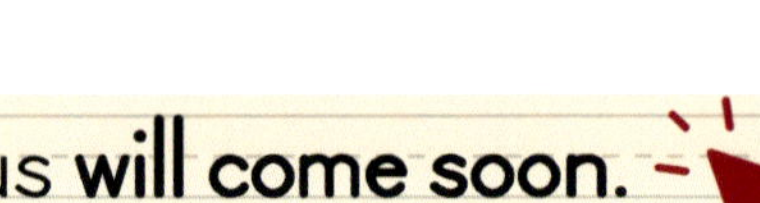

Now it's your turn. On the line that has a puppy in front of it, find the sentence that is next to the one we just read together. Put your pointer finger in front of the first word.

Let's review the steps:

1. **Look at each word and decide if it's a high-frequency word.**
   - **If the word is bold, it's a high-frequency word. Read the word.**
   - **If it's not a high-frequency word, point to the letters, say the sounds, and then read the word.**
2. **Continue until you read each word.**
3. **Then read the sentence.**

(After reading, ask the students what the person in the story is looking for. **The person is looking for a bag.**)

1. **I must find my** bag.
2. **Please look for** it.
3. **Where** did it **go**?

Writing

WRITE SENTENCES

Now we'll practice writing sentences.

Answer with me as we do the first one together.

Let's write the following sentence: We have no gas. Repeat it.
We have no gas. (Hold up 1 finger for each word as you repeat the sentence.)
- **How many words do you hear? 4**
- **What is the first word? We I write the high-frequency word spelled uppercase W, lowercase e.**
- (Repeat the sentence.) **What is the second word? have I write the high-frequency word spelled h-a-v-e.**
- (Repeat the sentence.) **What is the third word? no I write the high-frequency word spelled n-o.**
- (Repeat the sentence.) **What is the last word? gas**
  - **Sounds and letters? /g/ g - /ă/ a - /s/ s**
- **Punctuation mark? period**
- **Read the sentence. We have no gas.**

Now it's your turn. Turn to page 32 in your Student Workbook. Find the line that has a bird in front of it.

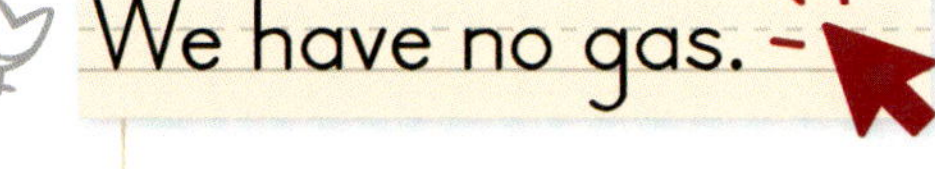

(Display word box.)
Above the line, there is a box that has some high-frequency words that we have learned. Let's read them together. please, must, soon, I, my

Here are the steps:
1. **I'll say the sentence and you repeat it.**
2. **I'll say each word, and before you write it, decide if it's a high-frequency word. Use the word boxes in your workbook to help you.**
   - **If it's a high-frequency word, write the letters.**
   - **If it's not a high-frequency word, break the word into sounds and write the letter for each sound.**

please, must, soon, I, my

1. Please get a cab.
2. It must come soon.
3. I must get to my job.

Day 18

3. Make sure the first letter in your sentence and all names are uppercase.
4. Put a punctuation mark at the end.
5. Then, read the sentence.

Now that you have written 3 sentences, go back to the top and trace the first sentence. Finally, whisper read all 4 sentences.

Phonological Awareness Wrap-Up

PHONOLOGICAL AWARENESS: PHONEME SEGMENTATION

Now, we are going to practice <u>segmenting phonemes</u> in words.

Let's review the instructions:
- I'll say a word and you repeat it.
- Then, I'll ask you to tell me the sounds in the word. Ready?

Say my: (my) Sounds?	/m/ /ī/	Say lie: (lie) Sounds?	/l/ /ī/
Say hi: (hi) Sounds?	/h/ /ī/	Say more: (more) Sounds?	/m/ /or/
Say bee: (bee) Sounds?	/b/ /ē/	Say she: (she) Sounds?	/sh/ /ē/
Say by: (by) Sounds?	/b/ /ī/	Say do: (do) Sounds?	/d/ /ū/
Say day: (day) Sounds?	/d/ /ā/	Say eat: (eat) Sounds?	/ē/ /t/
Say it: (it) Sounds?	/ĭ/ /t/	Say age: (age) Sounds?	/ā/ /j/
Say us: (us) Sounds?	/ŭ/ /s/	Say door: (door) Sounds?	/d/ /or/
Say he: (he) Sounds?	/h/ /ē/	Say key: (key) Sounds?	/k/ /ē/

DAY 19

Phonological Awareness Warm-Up

PHONOLOGICAL AWARENESS: PHONEME SEGMENTATION

Today we are going to practice <u>segmenting phonemes</u> in words.

Let's review the instructions:
- I'll say a word and you repeat it.
- Then, I'll ask you to tell me the sounds in the word. Ready?

Say lad: (lad) Sounds?	/l/ /ă/ /d/	Say shine: (shine) Sounds?	/sh/ /ī/ /n/
Say hut: (hut) Sounds?	/h/ /ŭ/ /t/	Say leg: (leg) Sounds?	/l/ /ĕ/ /g/
Say bet: (bet) Sounds?	/b/ /ĕ/ /t/	Say shed: (shed) Sounds?	/sh/ /ĕ/ /d/
Say sag: (sag) Sounds?	/s/ /ă/ /g/	Say dot: (dot) Sounds?	/d/ /ŏ/ /t/
Say dad: (dad) Sounds?	/d/ /ă/ /d/	Say meat: (meat) Sounds?	/m/ /ē/ /t/
Say cot: (cot) Sounds?	/k/ /ŏ/ /t/	Say page: (page) Sounds?	/p/ /ā/ /j/
Say bus: (bus) Sounds?	/b/ /ŭ/ /s/	Say dog: (dog) Sounds?	/d/ /ŏ/ /g/
Say head: (head) Sounds?	/h/ /ĕ/ /d/	Say whale: (whale) Sounds?	/hw/ /ā/ /l/

High-Frequency Words

Now I'm going to show you how to read 4 more high-frequency words. Watch me, my turn.

(Display <u>funny</u>.)
The word is <u>funny</u>, as in the sentence "My movie was funny."
- **Watch me finger-stretch the sounds. /f/ /ŭ/ /n/ /ē/** (Show thumb for /f/, pointer finger for /ŭ/, middle finger for /n/, and ring finger for /ē/.)
- **There are 4 sounds in the word** *funny*. **This word is spelled with 5 letters, *f-u-n-n-y*.**

Now it's your turn. Word? funny How many letters? 5
The letter names are f-u-n-n-y. Say them with me. f-u-n-n-y

(Use the process below to review the next 3 words.)

HFW List
pretty   /p/ /r/ /ĭ/ /t/ /ē/
came   /k/ /ā/ /m/
name   /n/ /ā/ /m/

- **The word is _______. What is the word? _______**
- **Listen for this word in the following sentence.** (Use the word in a sentence.)
- **Watch me finger-stretch the sounds.**
- **There are** (number) **sound(s) in the word _______.**
- **This word is spelled with** (number) **letter(s), _______.**

Now it's your turn.
- **Word? _______ How many letter(s)? _______**
- **The letter name(s) are _______. Say them with me. _______**

How are the words *came* and *name* alike? They both end in a-m-e. They rhyme.

FLUENCY: HIGH-FREQUENCY WORDS

Now we will practice reading the words we know.

(Display the high-frequency word grid. Prompt students by saying **"Word?"** at each box.)

funny	came	pretty	name
soon	under	well	all
help	must	please	new
out	will	went	where

Reading

READ A STORY

Now we will reread the story *As Good as New*.

Turn to page 27 in your workbook. Find the title of the story. Let's read it together. As Good as New

Now, find the first sentence of the story. Here are the steps:

1. Look at each word and decide if it's a high-frequency word.
   - If it's a high-frequency word, read the word.
   - If it's not a high-frequency word, point to the letters, say the sounds, and then read the word.
2. Use this routine to read all the sentences in the story.

We'll discuss the story when you've finished reading.

> **As Good as New**
> I am Rex and I have a hat.
> I hop and bop with my hat.
> I rap and tap with my hat.
> But now it has a rip.
> Kim said, "Get rid of it."
> I went to Yun.
> He said, "Let me see."
> In a bit, I got my hat.
> "Have a look," said Yun.
> I said, "It is as good as new."

(After reading, ask students what Kim thought should happen to the hat.
Kim thought Rex should get rid of the hat.)

Writing

WRITE SENTENCES

Now we'll practice writing sentences.

Answer with me as we do the first one together.

Let's write the following sentence: <u>Sal is a pretty gal.</u> Repeat it. **Sal is a pretty gal.** (Hold up 1 finger for each word as you repeat the sentence.)

- How many words do you hear? **5**
- What is the first word? **Sal**
  - Sounds and letters? **/s/ uppercase S - /ă/ a - /l/ l**
  - Notice that S is uppercase because it's the first word in a sentence and is the first letter of a name.
- (Repeat the sentence.) What is the second word? **is**
  I write the high-frequency word spelled i-s.
- (Repeat the sentence.) What is the third word? **a** I write the high-frequency word spelled a.
- (Repeat the sentence.) What is the fourth word? **pretty**
  I write the high-frequency word spelled p-r-e-t-t-y.
- (Repeat the sentence.) What is the last word? **gal**
  - Sounds and letters? **/g/ g - /ă/ a - /l/ l**
- Punctuation mark? **period**
- Read the sentence. **Sal is a pretty gal.**

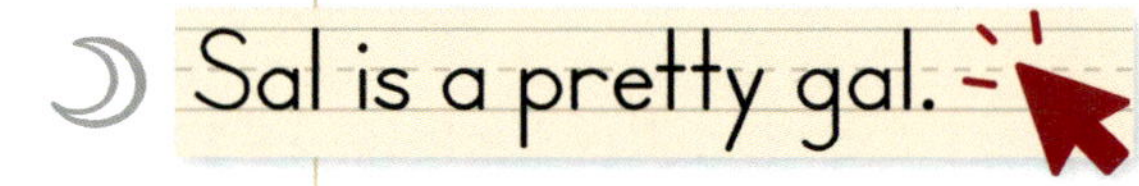

Now it's your turn. Turn to page 33 in your Student Workbook. Find the line that has a moon in front of it.

(Display word box.)

Above the line, there is a box that has some high-frequency words that we have learned. Let's read them together. she, funny, too, one

Here are the steps:
1. **I'll say the sentence and you repeat it.**
2. **I'll say each word, and before you write it, decide if it's a high-frequency word. Use the word boxes in your workbook to help you.**
   - **If it's a high-frequency word, write the letters.**
   - **If it's not a high-frequency word, break the word into sounds and write the letter for each sound.**
3. **Make sure the first letter in your sentence and all names are uppercase.**
4. **Put a punctuation mark at the end.**
5. **Then, read the sentence.**

Now that you have written 3 sentences, go back to the top and trace the first sentence. Finally, whisper read all 4 sentences.

she, funny, too, one

1. She is funny too.
2. She likes to tap one leg.
3. It looks like a jig.

Phonological Awareness Wrap-Up

PHONOLOGICAL AWARENESS: PHONEME SEGMENTATION

Now, we are going to practice <u>segmenting phonemes</u> in words.

Let's review the instructions:
- **I'll say a word and you repeat it.**
- **Then, I'll ask you to tell me the sounds in the word. Ready?**

Say bed: (bed) Sounds?	/b/ /ĕ/ /d/	Say pick: (pick) Sounds?	/p/ /ĭ/ /k/
Say hat: (hat) Sounds?	/h/ /ă/ /t/	Say leash: (leash) Sounds?	/l/ /ē/ /sh/
Say bite: (bite) Sounds?	/b/ /ī/ /t/	Say pig: (pig) Sounds?	/p/ /ĭ/ /g/
Say cage: (cage) Sounds?	/k/ /ā/ /j/	Say boat: (boat) Sounds?	/b/ /ō/ /t/
Say jack: (jack) Sounds?	/j/ /ă/ /k/	Say might: (might) Sounds?	/m/ /ī/ /t/
Say cheese: (cheese) Sounds?	/ch/ /ē/ /z/	Say hedge: (hedge) Sounds?	/h/ /ĕ/ /j/
Say bun: (bun) Sounds?	/b/ /ŭ/ /n/	Say bat: (bat) Sounds?	/b/ /ă/ /t/
Say dig: (dig) Sounds?	/d/ /ĭ/ /g/	Say wait: (wait) Sounds?	/w/ /ā/ /t/

Day **20**

DAY 20

Phonological Awareness Warm-Up

PHONOLOGICAL AWARENESS: PHONEME SEGMENTATION

Today we are going to practice segmenting phonemes in words.

Let's review the instructions:
- I'll say a word and you repeat it.
- Then, I'll ask you to tell me the sounds in the word. Ready?

Say chick: (chick) Sounds?	/ch/ /ĭ/ /k/	Say peck: (peck) Sounds?	/p/ /ĕ/ /k/
Say date: (date) Sounds?	/d/ /ā/ /t/	Say leap: (leap) Sounds?	/l/ /ē/ /p/
Say pop: (pop) Sounds?	/p/ /ŏ/ /p/	Say pan: (pan) Sounds?	/p/ /ă/ /n/
Say feel: (feel) Sounds?	/f/ /ē/ /l/	Say goat: (goat) Sounds?	/g/ /ō/ /t/
Say beach: (beach) Sounds?	/b/ /ē/ /ch/	Say wheel: (wheel) Sounds?	/hw/ /ē/ /l/
Say chat: (chat) Sounds?	/ch/ /ă/ /t/	Say red: (red) Sounds?	/r/ /ĕ/ /d/
Say bug: (bug) Sounds?	/b/ /ŭ/ /g/	Say vet: (vet) Sounds?	/v/ /ĕ/ /t/
Say have: (have) Sounds?	/h/ /ă/ /v/	Say well: (well) Sounds?	/w/ /ĕ/ /l/

Letter-Sound Correspondence

WORD COMPLETION WITH PICTURES

Now we're going to fill in the missing sound in words. Look at each picture. Fill in the correct letter to complete the word. After you write the letter, whisper read the word.

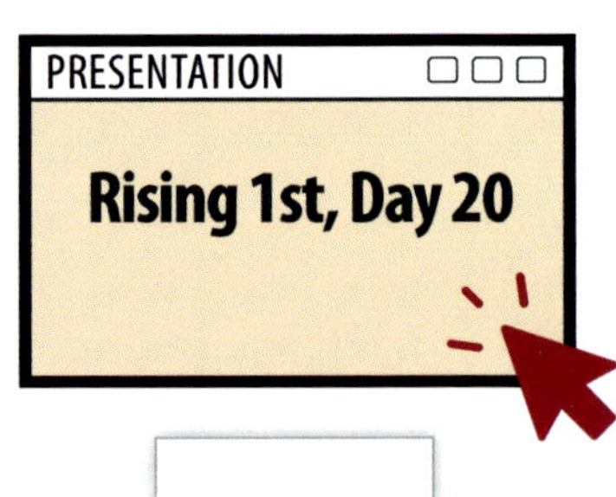

I'll do the first one. This picture is cab.
- I finger-stretch cab. /k/ /ă/ /b/
- I tap the letters and line while saying the sounds to see what sound is missing. (Tap the letter *c*, the line, and the letter *b*.)
  - The middle sound /ă/ is missing. The sound /ă/ is spelled with the letter *a*.
- Next, I write the letter *a* in the space.
- Finally, I slide a finger under the word and whisper "cab."

 Now it's your turn. Turn to page 33 in your Student Workbook. (Review the name of each picture with students before they begin.)

Here are the steps:
1. Finger-stretch the sounds.
2. Tap the letters and line while saying the sounds.
3. Write the letter for the missing sound.
4. Whisper read the word.

Answer Key

High-Frequency Words

Now I'm going to show you how to read 4 more high-frequency words. Watch me, my turn.

(Display black.)
The word is black, as in the sentence "The black cat has shiny eyes."
- **Watch me finger-stretch the sounds. /b/ /l/ /ă/ /k/** (Show thumb for /b/, pointer finger for /l/, middle finger for /ă/, and ring finger for /k/.)
- **There are 4 sounds in the word *black*. This word is spelled with 5 letters, *b-l-a-c-k*.**

Now it's your turn. Word? black How many letters? 5
The letter names are b-l-a-c-k. Say them with me. b-l-a-c-k

black

(Use the process below to review the next 3 words.)

HFW List	
blue /b/ /l/ /ū/	• **The word is ______. What is the word? ______** • **Listen for this word in the following sentence.** (Use the word in a sentence.) • **Watch me finger-stretch the sounds.** • **There are** (number) **sound(s) in the word ______.** • **This word is spelled with** (number) **letter(s), ______.**
yellow /y/ /ĕ/ /l/ /ō/	**Now it's your turn.** • **Word? ______ How many letter(s)? ______**
brown /b/ /r/ /ou/ /n/	• **The letter name(s) are ______. Say them with me. ______**

blue
yellow
brown

FLUENCY: HIGH-FREQUENCY WORDS

Now we will practice reading the words we know.

(Display the high-frequency word grid. Prompt students by saying **"Word?"** at each box.)

yellow	brown	blue	black
name	came	pretty	funny
where	soon	please	must
went	under	new	help

Day 20

Reading

READ SENTENCES

It's sentence time!

 **Turn to page 34 in your workbook. Find the line that has a snowflake in front of it.**

(Display word box.)
Above the line, there is a box with some high-frequency words that we have learned. Let's read them together. my, yellow, black, has, blue, with, pretty, brown, new

> my, yellow, black, has, blue, with, pretty, brown, new

(Display sentence.)
Now, put your pointer finger in front of the first word in the sentence. Let's read this first sentence together.
(Follow the same process from previous days. Read the bold high-frequency words and sound out the decodable words that are not bold.)

❄ My mug is yellow and black.

Now it's your turn. On the line that has a snowflake in front of it, find the sentence that is next to the one we just read together. Put your pointer finger in front of the first word.

Let's review the steps:
1. **Look at each word and decide if it's a high-frequency word.**
   - **If the word is bold, it's a high-frequency word. Read the word.**
   - **If it's not a high-frequency word, point to the letters, say the sounds, and then read the word.**
2. **Continue until you read each word.**
3. **Then read the sentence.**

(After reading, ask the students what the color of Yen's mug is. **Yen's mug is blue.**)

> 1. Yen **has a** big **blue** mug.
> 2. **The** mug **with black** dots **is pretty**.
> 3. **The brown** mug **is new**.

Writing

WRITE SENTENCES

Now we'll practice writing sentences.

Answer with me as we do the first one together.

Let's write the following sentence: A bat is black. Repeat it.
A bat is black. (Hold up 1 finger for each word as you repeat the sentence.)
- **How many words do you hear? 4**
- **What is the first word? A I write the high-frequency word spelled uppercase A. Notice that A is uppercase because it's the first word in the sentence.**
- (Repeat the sentence.) **What is the second word? bat**
   - **Sounds and letters? /b/ b - /ă/ a - /t/ t**

- (Repeat the sentence.) **What is the third word? is** I write the high-frequency word spelled i-s.
- (Repeat the sentence.) **What is the last word? black** I write the high-frequency word spelled b-l-a-c-k.
- **Punctuation mark? period**
- **Read the sentence. A bat is black.**

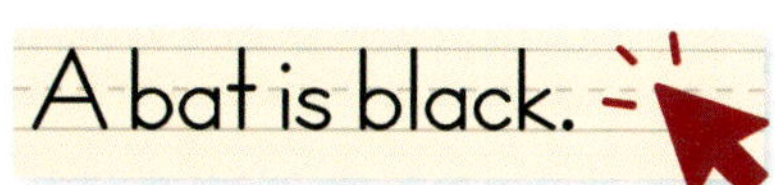

 Now it's your turn. Turn to page 34 in your Student Workbook. Find the line that has a bell in front of it.

(Display word box.)

Above the line, there is a box that has some high-frequency words that we have learned. Let's read them together. **blue, brown, yellow**

blue, brown, yellow

Here are the steps:
1. **I'll say the sentence and you repeat it.**
2. **I'll say each word, and before you write it, decide if it's a high-frequency word. Use the word boxes in your workbook to help you.**
   - **If it's a high-frequency word, write the letters.**
   - **If it's not a high-frequency word, break the word into sounds and write the letter for each sound.**
3. **Make sure the first letter in your sentence and all names are uppercase.**
4. **Put a punctuation mark at the end.**
5. **Then, read the sentence.**

1. The pen is blue.
2. Mud is brown.
3. The sun is yellow.

Now that you have written 3 sentences, go back to the top and trace the first sentence. Finally, whisper read all 4 sentences.

Phonological Awareness Wrap-Up

PHONOLOGICAL AWARENESS: PHONEME SEGMENTATION

Now, we are going to practice <u>segmenting phonemes</u> in words.

Let's review the instructions:
- **I'll say a word and you repeat it.**
- **Then, I'll ask you to tell me the sounds in the word. Ready?**

Say cheep: (cheep) Sounds?	/ch/ /ē/ /p/	Say tick: (tick) Sounds?	/t/ /ĭ/ /k/
Say dip: (dip) Sounds?	/d/ /ĭ/ /p/	Say move: (move) Sounds?	/m/ /ū/ /v/
Say bone: (bone) Sounds?	/b/ /ō/ /n/	Say duck: (duck) Sounds?	/d/ /ŭ/ /k/
Say peel: (peel) Sounds?	/p/ /ē/ /l/	Say coat: (coat) Sounds?	/k/ /ō/ /t/
Say rig: (rig) Sounds?	/r/ /ĭ/ /g/	Say home: (home) Sounds?	/h/ /ō/ /m/
Say vine: (vine) Sounds?	/v/ /ī/ /n/	Say kick: (kick) Sounds?	/k/ /ĭ/ /k/
Say boss: (boss) Sounds?	/b/ /ŏ/ /s/	Say nice: (nice) Sounds?	/n/ /ī/ /s/
Say love: (love) Sounds?	/l/ /ŭ/ /v/	Say bell: (bell) Sounds?	/b/ /ĕ/ /l/

Day 21

Days 21–25: Short Vowel, Reading, & Writing 4

Learning Objective

Students demonstrate understanding of how to read sentences and short stories with decodable VC and CVC words and selected irregularly spelled high-frequency words. Additionally, they write short sentences composed of these types of words.

DAY 21

Phonological Awareness Warm-Up

PHONOLOGICAL AWARENESS: INITIAL PHONEME SUBSTITUTION

Today we are going to practice <u>substituting, or changing, the beginning sound</u> in a word to make a new word.

Listen, watch me.
- The word is <u>cat</u>. I change /k/ to /b/: /b/ /ă/ /t/. The new word is bat.

Let's practice together.
- Say <u>may</u>: (may) Change /m/ to /s/. Word? say
- Say <u>man</u>: (man) Change /m/ to /r/. Word? ran

Now it's your turn. Here are the instructions:
- I'll say a word and you repeat it.
- Next, I'll tell you a sound to change in the word.
- Then, I'll ask you to tell me the new word.

Say miss: (miss) Change /m/ to /k/. Word?	kiss	Say bell: (bell) Change /b/ to /t/. Word?	tell
Say bark: (bark) Change /b/ to /m/. Word?	mark	Say bite: (bite) Change /b/ to /k/. Word?	kite
Say hat: (hat) Change /h/ to /k/. Word?	cat	Say show: (show) Change /sh/ to /t/. Word?	toe
Say dust: (dust) Change /d/ to /m/. Word?	must	Say far: (far) Change /f/ to /b/. Word?	bar
Say cob: (cob) Change /k/ to /s/. Word?	sob	Say cap: (cap) Change /k/ to /l/. Word?	lap
Say phone: (phone) Change /f/ to /b/. Word?	bone	Say same: (same) Change /s/ to /k/. Word?	came
Say book: (book) Change /b/ to /l/. Word?	look	Say fee: (fee) Change /f/ to /s/. Word?	see
Say cup: (cup) Change /k/ to /p/. Word?	pup	Say bird: (bird) Change /b/ to /th/. Word?	third

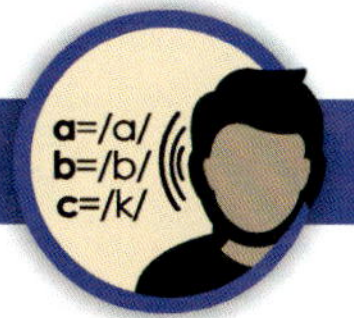

Letter-Sound Correspondence

WORD COMPLETION WITH PICTURES

Now we're going to fill in the missing sound in words. Look at each picture. Fill in the correct letter to complete the word. After you write the letter, whisper read the word.

I'll do the first one. This picture is <u>mop</u>.
- I finger-stretch mop. /m/ /ŏ/ /p/
- I tap the letters and line while saying the sounds to see what sound is missing. (Tap the line, the letter *o*, and the letter *p*.)
  - The first sound /m/ is missing. The sound /m/ is spelled with the letter *m*.
- Next, I write the letter *m* in the space.
- Finally, I slide a finger under the word and whisper "mop."

 **Now it's your turn. Turn to page 37 in your Student Workbook.** (Review the name of each picture with students before they begin.)

Here are the steps:
1. Finger-stretch the sounds.
2. Tap the letters and line while saying the sounds.
3. Write the letter for the missing sound.
4. Whisper read the word.

Answer Key

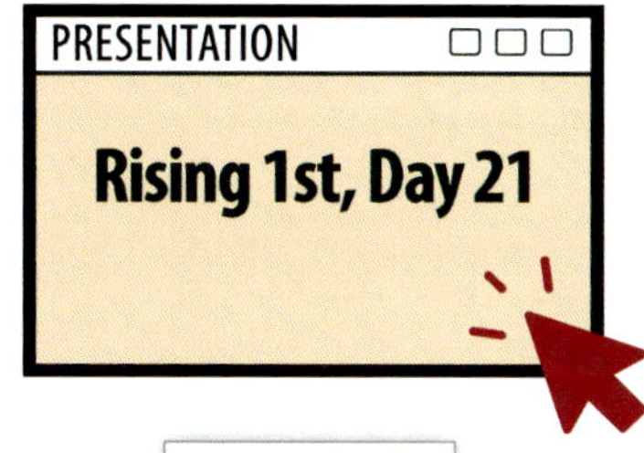

High-Frequency Words

Now I'm going to show you how to read 4 more high-frequency words. Watch me, my turn.

(Display <u>ate</u>.)

The word is <u>ate</u>, as in the sentence "I ate all my broccoli."
- **Watch me finger-stretch the sounds. /ā/ /t/** (Show thumb for /ā/ and pointer finger for /t/.)
- **There are 2 sounds in the word *ate*. This word is spelled with 3 letters, *a-t-e*.**

Now it's your turn. Word? ate How many letters? 3
The letter names are a-t-e. Say them with me. a-t-e

(Use the process below to review the next 3 words.)

ate

make
ride
white

HFW List	• The word is _______. What is the word? _______
make /m/ /ā/ /k/	• Listen for this word in the following sentence. (Use the word in a sentence.) • Watch me finger-stretch the sounds. • There are <u>(number)</u> sound(s) in the word _______.
ride /r/ /ī/ /d/	• This word is spelled with <u>(number)</u> letter(s), _______. Now it's your turn. • Word? _______ How many letter(s)? _______
white /hw/ /ī/ /t/	• The letter name(s) are _______. Say them with me. _______

Notice that all 4 high-frequency words today have long vowel sounds. Repeat them with me. ate, make, ride, white The words *ate* and *make* have the long a. The words *ride* and *white* have the long i. The silent letter *e* at the end works with the vowels *a* and *i* so these words are pronounced with the long vowel sound.

FLUENCY: HIGH-FREQUENCY WORDS

Now we will practice reading the words we know.

(Display the high-frequency word grid. Prompt students by saying **"Word?"** at each box.)

ride	make	ate	white
yellow	came	soon	where
name	brown	black	funny
must	please	pretty	blue

We know that the words *make* and *ate* have the long a vowel sound. Which other 2 words in the high-frequency word table have the long a vowel sound? came, name

Reading

READ SENTENCES

It's sentence time!

Turn to page 38 in your workbook. Find the line that has a rocket in front of it.

(Display word box.)
Above the line, there is a box with some high-frequency words that we have learned. Let's read them together. went, ride, he, will, make, ate, all

went, ride, he, will, make, ate, all

Now, put your pointer finger in front of the first word in the sentence.

(Display sentence.)
Let's read this first sentence together. (Follow the same process from previous days. Read the bold high-frequency words and sound out the decodable words that are not bold.)

Tom **went** on **a** ride.

Now it's your turn. On the line that has a rocket in front of it, find the sentence that is next to the one we just read together. Put your pointer finger in front of the first word.

Let's review the steps:
1. **Look at each word and decide if it's a high-frequency word.**
   - **If it is a bold word, it's a high-frequency word. Read the word.**
   - **If it's not a high-frequency word, point to the letters, say the sounds, and then read the word.**
2. **Continue until you read each word.**
3. **Then read the sentence.**

(After reading, ask the students what Tom made in a pan. **Tom made a ham in a pan.**)

1. **He went to** get **a** ham.
2. **He will make** it in **a** pan.
3. Tom **ate all the** ham.

Writing

WRITE SENTENCES

Now we'll practice writing sentences.

Answer with me as we do the first one together.

Let's write the following sentence: The bib is white. Repeat it.
The bib is white. (Hold up 1 finger for each word as you repeat the sentence.)
- **How many words do you hear? 4**
- (Repeat the sentence.) **What is the first word? The** I write the high-frequency word spelled uppercase T, lowercase h-e.
- (Repeat the sentence.) **What is the second word? bib**
   - **Sounds and letters? /b/ b - /ĭ/ i - /b/ b**
- (Repeat the sentence.) **What is the third word? is** I write the high-frequency word spelled i-s.

Day 21

- (Repeat the sentence.) **What is the last word? white**
  - **Sounds and letters? /hw/ wh - /ī/ i - /t/ t plus silent-e**
- **Punctuation mark? period**
- **Read the sentence. The bib is white.**

Now it's your turn. Turn to page 38 in your Student Workbook. Find the line that has a leaf in front of it.

(Display word box.)
Above the line, there is a box that has some high-frequency words that we have learned. Let's read them together. ate, white, has, make

Here are the steps:
1. **I'll say the sentence and you repeat it.**
2. **I'll say each word, and before you write it, decide if it's a high-frequency word. Use the word boxes in your workbook to help you.**
   - **If it's a high-frequency word, write the letters.**
   - **If it's not a high-frequency word, break the word into sounds and write the letter for each sound.**
3. **Make sure the first letter in your sentence and all names are uppercase.**
4. **Put a punctuation mark at the end.**
5. **Then, read the sentence.**

Now that you have written 3 sentences, go back to the top and trace the first sentence. Finally, whisper read all 4 sentences.

ate, white, has, make

1. The tot ate a red yam.
2. The white bib has a red dot.
3. Get it wet to make it white.

Phonological Awareness Wrap-Up

PHONOLOGICAL AWARENESS: INITIAL PHONEME SUBSTITUTION

Now, we are going to practice <u>substituting</u>, or changing, the <u>beginning sound</u> in a word to make a new word. Let's review the instructions:
- **I'll say a word and you repeat it.**
- **Next, I'll tell you a sound to change in the word.**
- **Then, I'll ask you to tell me the new word.**

Say said: (said) Change /s/ to /b/. Word?	bed	Say lip: (lip) Change /l/ to /s/. Word?	sip
Say back: (back) Change /b/ to /p/. Word?	pack	Say hear: (hear) Change /h/ to /f/. Word?	fear
Say get: (get) Change /g/ to /m/. Word?	met	Say gum: (gum) Change /g/ to /h/. Word?	hum
Say bad: (bad) Change /b/ to /s/. Word?	sad	Say cop: (cop) Change /k/ to /ch/. Word?	chop
Say pole: (pole) Change /p/ to /h/. Word?	hole	Say house: (house) Change /h/ to /m/. Word?	mouse
Say too: (too) Change /t/ to /sh/. Word?	shoe	Say fill: (fill) Change /f/ to /p/. Word?	pill
Say bike: (bike) Change /b/ to /l/. Word?	like	Say mug: (mug) Change /m/ to /b/. Word?	bug
Say bull: (bull) Change /b/ to /p/. Word?	pull	Say way: (way) Change /w/ to /l/. Word?	lay

DAY 22

Phonological Awareness Warm-Up

PHONOLOGICAL AWARENESS: INITIAL PHONEME SUBSTITUTION

Today we are going to practice substituting, or changing, the beginning sound in a word to make a new word. Let's review the instructions:

- I'll say a word and you repeat it.
- Next, I'll tell you a sound to change in the word.
- Then, I'll ask you to tell me the new word.

Say row: (row) Change /r/ to /m/. Word?	mow	Say lace: (lace) Change /l/ to /f/. Word?	face
Say cop: (cop) Change /k/ to /t/. Word?	top	Say room: (room) Change /r/ to /b/. Word?	boom
Say feet: (feet) Change /f/ to /m/. Word?	meet	Say lid: (lid) Change /l/ to /k/. Word?	kid
Say sip: (sip) Change /s/ to /z/. Word?	zip	Say fed: (fed) Change /f/ to /l/. Word?	led
Say peach: (peach) Change /p/ to /b/. Word?	beach	Say zoo: (zoo) Change /z/ to /m/. Word?	moo
Say sit: (sit) Change /s/ to /p/. Word?	pit	Say corn: (corn) Change /k/ to /b/. Word?	born
Say lash: (lash) Change /l/ to /k/. Word?	cash	Say pool: (pool) Change /p/ to /t/. Word?	tool
Say mail: (mail) Change /m/ to /n/. Word?	nail	Say late: (late) Change /l/ to /w/. Word?	wait

High-Frequency Words

Now we will practice reading some of our previously reviewed high-frequency words.

- (Display are.) **This is the word** *are,* **as in "Are you going to the game?" Repeat the word** *are.* are
- (Display go.) **This is the word** *go,* **as in "Let's go see a movie." Repeat the word** *go.* go
- (Display have.) **This is the word** *have,* **as in "We have a dog." Repeat the word** *have.* have
- (Display say.) **This is the word** *say,* **as in "Say the alphabet." Repeat the word** *say.* say
- (Display with.) **This is the word** *with,* **as in "Can I go with you?" Repeat the word** *with.* with

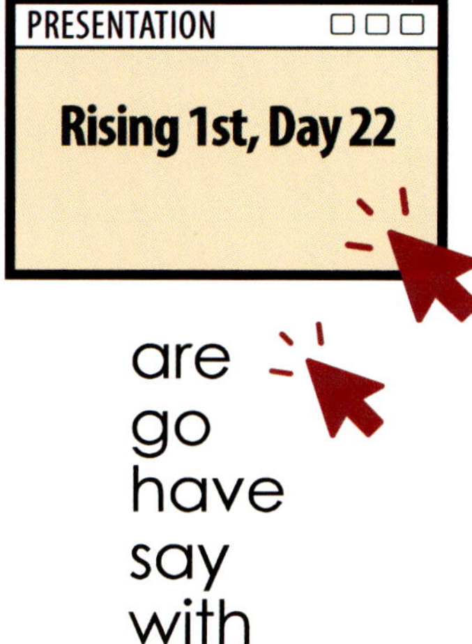

FLUENCY: HIGH-FREQUENCY WORDS

Now we will practice reading the words we know.

(Display the high-frequency word grid. Prompt students by saying **"Word?"** at each box.)

have	with	are	go
say	no	little	we
now	my	what	good
this	yes	jump	me

Reading

READ A STORY

Now, let's read a story.

 **Turn to page 35 in your workbook. Find the title of the story. Let's read it together. The Pet Doc This story is about Ana. Ana is spelled uppercase A-n-a. Can you point to the name Ana in the story? Say her name with me. Ana**

Now, find the first sentence of the story. Here are the steps:
  1. **Look at each word and decide if it's a high-frequency word.**
     – **If it's a high-frequency word, read the word.**
     – **If it's not a high-frequency word, point to the letters, say the sounds, and then read the word.**
  2. **Use this routine to read all the sentences in the story.**
  3. **After you read the story, we will read it together.**

> **The Pet Doc**
> My name is Ana.
> I am a doc.
> My job is to help pets.
> I see hens, hogs, cats, and dogs.
> This is Max, a big black ram.
> Max is sad and is not well.
> I dab a hot rag on his hip.
> Soon Max will run and jump.
> Now I must go help a pup.
> It is good to be a vet.

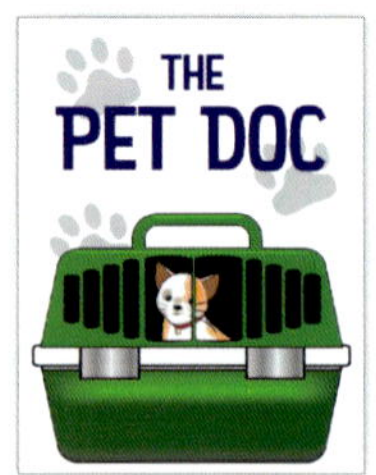

(After reading, ask students what job Ana has. **Ana is a vet. She helps pets.**)

Writing

WRITE SENTENCES

Now we'll practice writing sentences.

Answer with me as we do the first one together.

Let's write the following sentence: <u>We are at the lot.</u> Repeat it.
We are at the lot. (Hold up 1 finger for each word as you repeat the sentence.)
- **How many words do you hear? 5**
- **What is the first word? We I write the high-frequency word spelled uppercase W, lowercase e.**
- **(Repeat the sentence.) What is the second word? are I write the high-frequency word spelled a-r-e.**
- **(Repeat the sentence.) What is the third word? at**
  - **Sounds and letters? /ă/ a - /t/ t**
- **(Repeat the sentence.) What is the fourth word? the I write the high-frequency word spelled t-h-e.**
- **(Repeat the sentence.) What is the fifth word? lot**
  - **Sounds and letters? /l/ l - /ŏ/ o - /t/ t**
- **Punctuation mark? period**
- **Read the sentence. We are at the lot.**

 **Now it's your turn. Turn to page 39 in your Student Workbook. Find the line that has an umbrella in front of it.**

(Display word box.)
Above the line, there is a box with some high-frequency words that we have learned. Let's read them together. I, say, we, help

Here are the steps:
1. **I'll say the sentence and you repeat it.**
2. **I'll say each word, and before you write it, decide if it's a high-frequency word. Use the word boxes in your workbook to help you.**
   - **If it's a high-frequency word, write the letters.**
   - **If it's not a high-frequency word, break the word into sounds and write the letter for each sound.**
3. **Make sure the first letter in your sentence and all names are uppercase.**
4. **Put a punctuation mark at the end.**
5. **Then, read the sentence.**

Now that you have written 2 sentences, go back to the top and trace the first sentence. Finally, whisper read all 3 sentences.

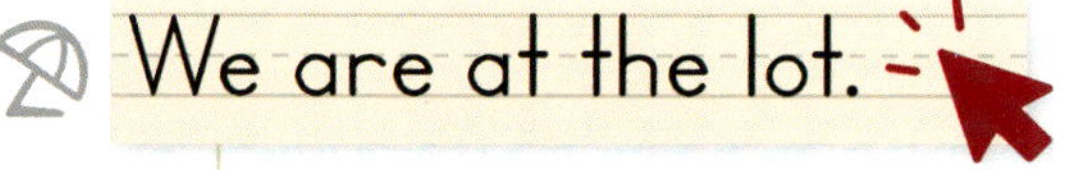

I, say, we, help

1. I say we dig a pit.
2. Can you help?

Day 22

Phonological Awareness Wrap-Up

PHONOLOGICAL AWARENESS: INITIAL PHONEME SUBSTITUTION

Now, we are going to practice substituting, or changing, the beginning sound in a word to make a new word. Let's review the instructions:

- I'll say a word and you repeat it.
- Next, I'll tell you a sound to change in the word.
- Then, I'll ask you to tell me the new word.

Say hair: (hair) Change /h/ to /b/. Word?	bear		Say pain: (pain) Change /p/ to /l/. Word?	lane
Say toss: (toss) Change /t/ to /b/. Word?	boss		Say cool: (cool) Change /k/ to /p/. Word?	pool
Say booth: (booth) Change /b/ to /t/. Word?	tooth		Say bake: (bake) Change /b/ to /r/. Word?	rake
Say ship: (ship) Change /sh/ to /d/. Word?	dip		Say pick: (pick) Change /p/ to /s/. Word?	sick
Say walk: (walk) Change /w/ to /ch/. Word?	chalk		Say go: (go) Change /g/ to /b/. Word?	bow
Say pay: (pay) Change /p/ to /d/. Word?	day		Say nose: (nose) Change /n/ to /h/. Word?	hose
Say sore: (sore) Change /s/ to /p/. Word?	pour		Say wife: (wife) Change /w/ to /n/. Word?	knife
Say care: (care) Change /k/ to /f/. Word?	fair		Say bead: (bead) Change /b/ to /n/. Word?	need

DAY 23

Phonological Awareness Warm-Up

PHONOLOGICAL AWARENESS: INITIAL PHONEME SUBSTITUTION

Today we are going to practice substituting, or changing, the beginning sound in a word to make a new word. Let's review the instructions:

- I'll say a word and you repeat it.
- Next, I'll tell you a sound to change in the word.
- Then, I'll ask you to tell me the new word.

Say sir: (sir) Change /s/ to /f/. Word?	fur		Say dog: (dog) Change /d/ to /h/. Word?	hog
Say bunch: (bunch) Change /b/ to /l/. Word?	lunch		Say map: (map) Change /m/ to /t/. Word?	tap
Say dug: (dug) Change /d/ to /j/. Word?	jug		Say lake: (lake) Change /l/ to /k/. Word?	cake
Say ship: (ship) Change /sh/ to /n/. Word?	nip		Say fine: (fine) Change /f/ to /l/. Word?	line
Say sigh: (sigh) Change /s/ to /p/. Word?	pie		Say ray: (ray) Change /r/ to /b/. Word?	bay
Say bob: (bob) Change /b/ to /j/. Word?	job		Say low: (low) Change /l/ to /b/. Word?	bow
Say fort: (fort) Change /f/ to /sh/. Word?	short		Say page: (page) Change /p/ to /k/. Word?	cage
Say soak: (soak) Change /s/ to /p/. Word?	poke		Say rat: (rat) Change /r/ to /m/. Word?	mat

Day
23

Letter-Sound Correspondence

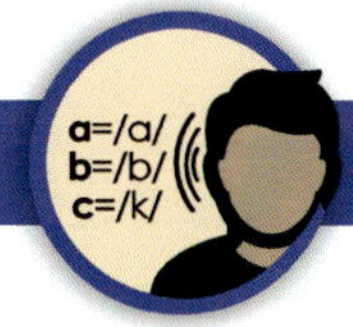

WORD COMPLETION WITH PICTURES

Now we're going to fill in the missing sound in words. Look at each picture. Fill in the correct letter to complete the word. After you write the letter, whisper read the word.

I'll do the first one. This picture is <u>d</u>ot.

- I finger-stretch dot. /d/ /ŏ/ /t/
- I tap the letters and line while saying the sounds to see what sound is missing. (Tap the line, the letter *o*, and the letter *t*.)
  - The first sound /d/ is missing. The sound /d/ is spelled with the letter *d*.
- Next, I write the letter *d* in the space.
- Finally, I slide a finger under the word and whisper "dot."

Now it's your turn. Turn to page 39 in your Student Workbook.
(Review the name of each picture with students before they begin.)

Here are the steps:
1. **Finger-stretch the sounds.**
2. **Tap the letters and line while saying the sounds.**
3. **Write the letter for the missing sound.**
4. **Whisper read the word.**

Answer Key

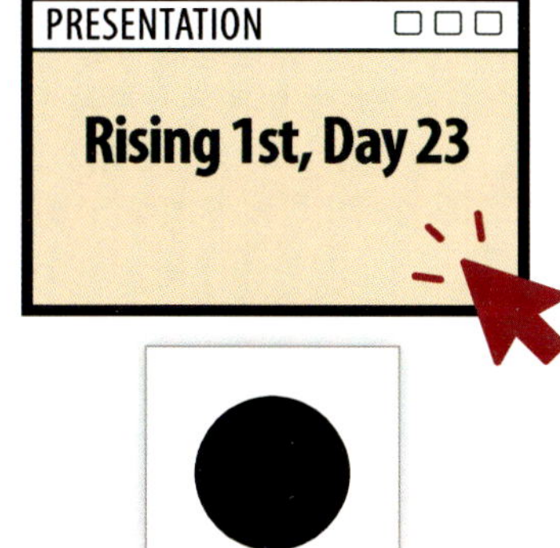

High-Frequency Words

Now we will practice reading some of our previously reviewed high-frequency words.

- (Display <u>has</u>.) **This is the word *has*, as in "She has blue eyes." Repeat the word *has*.** has
- (Display <u>down</u>.) **This is the word *down*, as in "We rode down the hill." Repeat the word *down*.** down
- (Display <u>he</u>.) **This is the word *he*, as in "He is tall." Repeat the word *he*.** he
- (Display <u>find</u>.) **This is the word *find*, as in "Can you find the ball?" Repeat the word *find*.** find
- (Display <u>play</u>.) **This is the word *play*, as in "Let's play outside." Repeat the word *play*.** play

has
down
he
find
play

FLUENCY: HIGH-FREQUENCY WORDS

Now we will practice reading the words we know.

(Display the high-frequency word grid. Prompt students by saying **"Word?"** at each box.)

he	play	has	find
down	I	be	so
his	as	that	she
eat	of	too	was

Reading

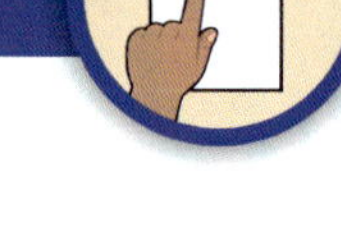

READ SENTENCES

It's sentence time!

 **Turn to page 40 in your workbook. Find the line that has cherries in front of it.**

(Display word box.)
Above the line, there is a box with some high-frequency words that we have learned. Let's read them together. find, white, he, pretty **Now, put your pointer finger in front of the first word in the sentence.**

find, white, he, pretty

Let's review the steps:
1. **Look at each word and decide if it's a high-frequency word.**
   - **If it is a bold word, it's a high-frequency word. Read the word.**
   - **If it's not a high-frequency word, point to the letters, say the sounds, and then read the word.**
2. **Continue until you read each word.**
3. **Then read the sentence.**

1. Deb **and** Viv **find a** den.
2. **They find a** fox in **the** den.
3. **The** fox **is** red **and white**.
4. **He is a pretty** fox.

(After reading, ask students where Deb and Viv find the fox. Deb and Viv find the fox in a den.)

Writing

WRITE SENTENCES

Now we'll practice writing sentences.

Answer with me as we do the first one together.

Let's write the following sentence: <u>Peg has a mix with nuts.</u> Repeat it. **Peg has a mix with nuts.** (Hold up 1 finger for each word as you repeat the sentence.)

- **How many words do you hear? 6**
- **What is the first word? Peg**
  - **Sounds and letters? /p/ uppercase P - /ĕ/ e - /g/ g**
- (Repeat the sentence.) **What is the second word? has I write the high-frequency word spelled h-a-s.**
- (Repeat the sentence.) **What is the third word? a I write the high-frequency word spelled a.**
- (Repeat the sentence.) **What is the fourth word? mix**
  - **Sounds and letters? /m/ m - /ĭ/ i - /k/ /s/ x**
- (Repeat the sentence.) **What is the fifth word? with I write the high-frequency word spelled w-i-t-h.**
- (Repeat the sentence.) **What is the last word? nuts**
  - **Sounds and letters? /n/ n - /ŭ/ u - /t/ t - /s/ s**
- **Punctuation mark? period**
- **Read the sentence. Peg has a mix with nuts.**

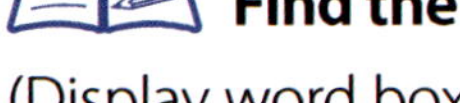

Now it's your turn. Turn to page 40 in your Student Workbook. Find the line that has a shirt in front of it.

(Display word box.)

Above the line, there is a box that has some high-frequency words that we have learned. Let's read them together. she, down, has, now, he

Here are the steps:
1. **I'll say the sentence and you repeat it.**
2. **I'll say each word, and before you write it, decide if it's a high-frequency word. Use the word boxes in your workbook to help you.**
   - **If it's a high-frequency word, write the letters.**
   - **If it's not a high-frequency word, break the word into sounds and write the letter for each sound.**
3. **Make sure the first letter in your sentence and all names are uppercase.**
4. **Put a punctuation mark at the end.**
5. **Then, read the sentence.**

Now that you have written 3 sentences, go back to the top and trace the first sentence. Finally, whisper re ad all 4 sentences.

she, down, has, now, he

1. She set it down.
2. Tad has it now.
3. He likes the mix.

Day **23**

Phonological Awareness Wrap-Up

PHONOLOGICAL AWARENESS: INITIAL PHONEME SUBSTITUTION

Now, we are going to practice <u>substituting, or changing, the beginning sound</u> in a word to make a new word. Let's review the instructions:

- I'll say a word and you repeat it.
- Next, I'll tell you a sound to change in the word.
- Then, I'll ask you to tell me the new word.

Say pork: (pork) Change /p/ to /f/. Word?	fork	Say nurse: (nurse) Change /n/ to /p/. Word?	purse
Say mice: (mice) Change /m/ to /d/. Word?	dice	Say sick: (sick) Change /s/ to /l/. Word?	lick
Say self: (self) Change /s/ to /sh/. Word?	shelf	Say pot: (pot) Change /p/ to /k/. Word?	cot
Say pan: (pan) Change /p/ to /t/. Word?	tan	Say big: (big) Change /b/ to /r/. Word?	rig
Say tub: (tub) Change /t/ to /k/. Word?	cub	Say red: (red) Change /r/ to /b/. Word?	bed
Say call: (call) Change /k/ to /t/. Word?	tall	Say fit: (fit) Change /f/ to /k/. Word?	kit
Say set: (set) Change /s/ to /l/. Word?	let	Say leg: (leg) Change /l/ to /p/. Word?	peg
Say so: (so) Change /s/ to /n/. Word?	no	Say ride: (ride) Change /r/ to /h/. Word?	hide

DAY 24

Phonological Awareness Warm-Up

PHONOLOGICAL AWARENESS: INITIAL PHONEME SUBSTITUTION

Now, we are going to practice <u>substituting, or changing, the beginning sound</u> to make a new word. Let's review the instructions:
- I'll say a word and you repeat it.
- Next, I'll tell you a sound to change in the word.
- Then, I'll ask you to tell me the new word.

Say hole: (hole) Change /h/ to /b/. Word?	bowl	Say car: (car) Change /k/ to /j/. Word?	jar
Say men: (men) Change /m/ to /t/. Word?	ten	Say mild: (mild) Change /m/ to /ch/. Word?	child
Say shell: (shell) Change /sh/ to /b/. Word?	bell	Say see: (see) Change /s/ to /w/. Word?	we
Say fun: (fun) Change /f/ to /s/. Word?	sun	Say were: (were) Change /w/ to /h/. Word?	her
Say mess: (mess) Change /m/ to /g/. Word?	guess	Say door: (door) Change /d/ to /m/. Word?	more
Say when: (when) Change /w/ to /d/. Word?	den	Say pen: (pen) Change /p/ to /h/. Word?	hen
Say mine: (mine) Change /m/ to /f/. Word?	fine	Say heard: (heard) Change /h/ to /b/. Word?	bird
Say pass: (pass) Change /p/ to /g/. Word?	gas	Say bag: (bag) Change /b/ to /w/. Word?	wag

High-Frequency Words

Now we will practice reading some of our previously reviewed high-frequency words.

- (Display <u>away</u>.) **This is the word *away*, as in "The bird flew away."** **Repeat the word *away*.** away
- (Display <u>here</u>.) **This is the word *here*, as in "Here is your snack."** **Repeat the word *here*.** here
- (Display <u>our</u>.) **This is the word *our*, as in "That is our house." Repeat the word *our*.** our
- (Display <u>saw</u>.) **This is the word *saw*, as in "I saw the rainbow."** **Repeat the word *saw*.** saw
- (Display <u>into</u>.) **This is the word *into*, as in "We went into the school."** **Repeat the word *into*.** into

FLUENCY: HIGH-FREQUENCY WORDS

Now we will practice reading the words we know.

(Display the high-frequency word grid. Prompt students by saying **"Word?"** at each box.)

our	into	away	here
saw	where	help	pretty
well	out	all	new
went	will	under	must

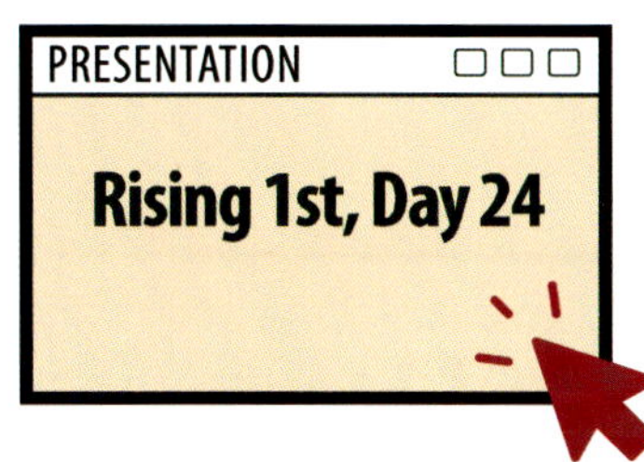

Reading

READ A STORY

Now we will reread the story *The Pet Doc*.

Turn to page 35 in your workbook. Find the title of the story. Let's read it together. The Pet Doc

Now, find the first sentence of the story. Here are the steps:

1. **Look at each word and decide if it's a high-frequency word.**
   - **If it's a high-frequency word, read the word.**
   - **If it's not a high-frequency word, point to the letters, say the sounds, and then read the word.**
2. **Use this routine to read all the sentences in the story.**

We'll discuss the story when you've finished reading.

Day 24

> **The Pet Doc**
>
> My name is Ana.
> I am a doc.
> My job is to help pets.
> I see hens, hogs, cats, and dogs.
> This is Max, a big black ram.
> Max is sad and is not well.
> I dab a hot rag on his hip.
> Soon Max will run and jump.
> Now I must go help a pup.
> It is good to be a vet.

(After reading, ask students why Max is sad. **Max does not feel well. Max hurt his hip.**)

Writing

WRITE SENTENCES

Now we'll practice writing sentences.

Answer with me as we do the first one together.

Let's write the following sentence: Pat is our hog. Repeat it.
Pat is our hog. (Hold up 1 finger for each word as you repeat the sentence.)

- **How many words do you hear? 4**
- **What is the first word? Pat**
  - **Sounds and letters? /p/ uppercase P - /ă/ a - /t/ t**
- (Repeat the sentence.) **What is the second word? is** I write the high-frequency word spelled i-s.
- (Repeat the sentence.) **What is the third word? our** I write the high-frequency word spelled o-u-r.
- (Repeat the sentence.) **What is the fourth word? hog**
  - **Sounds and letters? /h/ h - /ŏ/ o - /g/ g**
- **Punctuation mark? period**
- **Read the sentence. Pat is our hog.**

Day
24

Now it's your turn. Turn to page 41 in your Student Workbook. Find the line that has a box in front of it.

(Display word box.)

Above the line, there is a box that has some high-frequency words that we have learned. Let's read them together. he, away, into, brown, now

he, away, into, brown, now

Here are the steps:

1. **I'll say the sentence and you repeat it.**
2. **I'll say each word, and before you write it, decide if it's a high-frequency word. Use the word boxes in your workbook to help you.**
   - **If it's a high-frequency word, write the letters.**
   - **If it's not a high-frequency word, break the word into sounds and write the letter for each sound.**
3. **Make sure the first letter in your sentence and all names are uppercase.**
4. **Put a punctuation mark at the end.**
5. **Then, read the sentence.**

1. He ran away.   2. He ran into the mud.   3. Pat is a brown hog now.

Now that you have written 3 sentences, go back to the top and trace the first sentence. Finally, whisper read all 4 sentences.

Phonological Awareness Wrap-Up

PHONOLOGICAL AWARENESS: INITIAL PHONEME SUBSTITUTION

Now, we are going to practice substituting, or changing, the beginning sound to make a new word. Let's review the instructions:
- **I'll say a word and you repeat it.**
- **Next, I'll tell you a sound to change in the word.**
- **Then, I'll ask you to tell me the new word.**

Say mean: (mean) Change /m/ to /b/. Word?	bean	Say near: (near) Change /n/ to /t/. Word?	tear
Say night: (night) Change /n/ to /f/. Word?	fight	Say pad: (pad) Change /p/ to /m/. Word?	mad
Say gap: (gap) Change /g/ to /m/. Word?	map	Say give: (give) Change /g/ to /l/. Word?	live
Say sand: (sand) Change /s/ to /h/. Word?	hand	Say will: (will) Change /w/ to /ch/. Word?	chill
Say week: (week) Change /w/ to /b/. Word?	beak	Say my: (my) Change /m/ to /w/. Word?	why
Say ham: (ham) Change /h/ to /j/. Word?	jam	Say where: (where) Change /w/ to /sh/. Word?	share
Say tab: (tab) Change /t/ to /l/. Word?	lab	Say fin: (fin) Change /f/ to /w/. Word?	win
Say pet: (pet) Change /p/ to /j/. Word?	jet	Say chat: (chat) Change /ch/ to /b/. Word?	bat

DAY 25

Phonological Awareness Warm-Up

PHONOLOGICAL AWARENESS: INITIAL PHONEME SUBSTITUTION

Today we are going to practice <u>substituting, or changing, the</u> <u>beginning sound</u> to make a new word. Let's review the instructions:
- I'll say a word and you repeat it.
- Next, I'll tell you a sound to change in the word.
- Then, I'll ask you to tell me the new word.

Say keep: (keep) Change /k/ to /d/. Word?	**deep**	Say game: (game) Change /g/ to /f/. Word?	**fame**
Say hose: (hose) Change /h/ to /t/. Word?	**toes**	Say luck: (luck) Change /l/ to /b/. Word?	**buck**
Say log: (log) Change /l/ to /j/. Word?	**jog**	Say chop: (chop) Change /ch/ to /m/. Word?	**mop**
Say meal: (meal) Change /m/ to /f/. Word?	**feel**	Say cat: (cat) Change /k/ to /h/. Word?	**hat**
Say lime: (lime) Change /l/ to /d/. Word?	**dime**	Say coat: (coat) Change /k/ to /g/. Word?	**goat**
Say can: (can) Change /k/ to /r/. Word?	**ran**	Say tea: (tea) Change /t/ to /s/. Word?	**see**
Say base: (base) Change /b/ to /r/. Word?	**race**	Say fun: (fun) Change /f/ to /b/. Word?	**bun**
Say by: (by) Change /b/ to /sh/. Word?	**shy**	Say rack: (rack) Change /r/ to /b/. Word?	**back**

Letter-Sound Correspondence

WORD COMPLETION WITH PICTURES

Now we're going to fill in the missing sound in words. Look at each picture. Fill in the correct letter to complete the word. After you write the letter, whisper read the word.

I'll do the first one. This picture is <u>cop</u>.
- I finger-stretch cop. /k/ /ŏ/ /p/
- I tap the letters and line while saying the sounds to see what sound is missing. (Tap the letter *c*, the line, and the letter *p*.)
  - The middle sound /ŏ/ is missing. The sound /ŏ/ is spelled with the letter *o*.
- Next, I write the letter *o* in the space.
- Finally, I slide a finger under the word and whisper "cop."

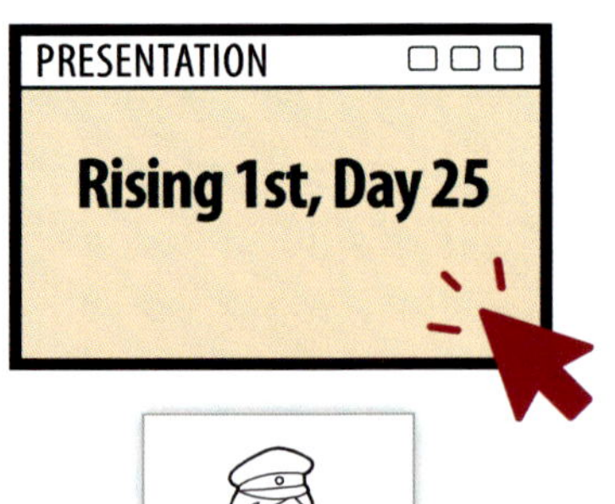

 **Now it's your turn. Turn to page 41 in your Student Workbook.** (Review the name of each picture with students before they begin.)

Here are the steps:
1. Finger-stretch the sounds.
2. Tap the letters and line while saying the sounds.
3. Write the letter for the missing sound.
4. Whisper read the word.

Answer Key

d <u>i</u> g	<u>n</u> et	we <u>b</u>	f <u>o</u> x
<u>l</u> og	m <u>u</u> g	d <u>a</u> d	<u>p</u> en

High-Frequency Words

Now we will practice reading some of our previously reviewed high-frequency words.

- (Display <u>there</u>.) **This is the word *there*, as in "Sit over there." Repeat the word *there*.** there
- (Display <u>one</u>.) **This is the word *one*, as in "I have one pencil." Repeat the word *one*.** one
- (Display <u>please</u>.) **This is the word *please*, as in "Please help your friend." Repeat the word *please*.** please
- (Display <u>soon</u>.) **This is the word *soon*, as in "The train will come soon." Repeat the word *soon*.** soon
- (Display <u>came</u>.) **This is the word *came*, as in "He came to my game." Repeat the word *came*.** came

there

one

please

soon

came

FLUENCY: HIGH-FREQUENCY WORDS

Now we will practice reading the words we know.

(Display the high-frequency word grid. Prompt students by saying **"Word?"** at each box.)

one	came	soon	please
there	two	black	funny
make	yellow	four	brown
three	blue	ate	white

Reading

READ SENTENCES

It's sentence time!

 **Turn to page 42 in your workbook. Find the line that has a paw print in front of it.**

(Display word box.)

Above the line, there is a box with some high-frequency words that we have learned. Let's read them together. there, with, please, out, I, soon, was, of **Now, put your pointer finger in front of the first word in the sentence.**

there, with, please, out, I, soon, was, of

Let's review the steps:
1. **Look at each word and decide if it's a high-frequency word.**
   – **If the word is bold, it's a high-frequency word. Read the word.**
   – **If it's not a high-frequency word, point to the letters, say the sounds, and then read the word.**
2. **Continue until you read each word.**
3. **Then read the sentence.**

1. **There is a** bug **with a** web in **the** tub.
2. Sis **said,** "**Please** get it **out**."
3. **I** can get it **with a** net.
4. **Soon the** bug **was out of the** tub.

(After reading, ask students what was in the tub. A bug with a web was in the tub.)

Writing

WRITE SENTENCES

Now we'll practice writing sentences.

Answer with me as we do the first one together.

Let's write the following sentence: Jeb has gum. **Repeat it.** Jeb has gum.
(Hold up 1 finger for each word as you repeat the sentence.)
- **How many words do you hear?** 3
- **What is the first word?** Jeb
  – **Sounds and letters?** /j/ uppercase J - /ĕ/ e - /b/ b
- (Repeat the sentence.) **What is the second word?** has I write the high-frequency word spelled h-a-s.
- (Repeat the sentence.) **What is the third word?** gum
  – **Sounds and letters?** /g/ g - /ŭ/ u - /m/ m
- **Punctuation mark?** period
- **Read the sentence.** Jeb has gum.

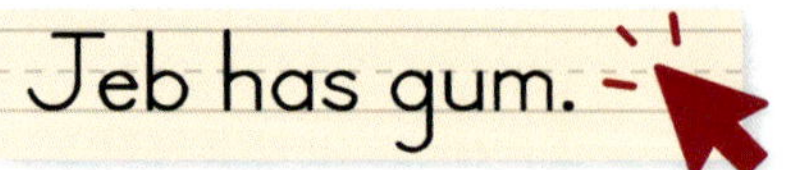

Day
25

Now it's your turn. Turn to page 42 in your Student Workbook. Find the line that has a shopping cart in front of it.

(Display word box.)

Above the line, there is a box that has some high-frequency words that we have learned. Let's read them together. I, please, have, one, my, good

I, please, have, one, my, good

Here are the steps:
1. **I'll say the sentence and you repeat it.**
2. **I'll say each word, and before you write it, decide if it's a high-frequency word. Use the word boxes in your workbook to help you.**
   - **If it's a high-frequency word, write the letters.**
   - **If it's not a high-frequency word, break the word into sounds and write the letter for each sound.**
3. **Make sure the first letter in your sentence and all names are uppercase.**
4. **Put a punctuation mark at the end.**
5. **Then, read the sentence.**

Now that you have written 3 sentences, go back to the top and trace the first sentence. Finally, whisper read all 4 sentences.

1. Can I please have one? 2. I can pop my gum. 3. Gum is good.

Phonological Awareness Wrap-Up

PHONOLOGICAL AWARENESS: INITIAL PHONEME SUBSTITUTION

Now, we are going to practice substituting, or changing, the beginning sound to make a new word. Let's review the instructions:
- **I'll say a word and you repeat it.**
- **Next, I'll tell you a sound to change in the word.**
- **Then, I'll ask you to tell me the new word.**

Say dive: (dive) Change /d/ to /h/. Word?	hive	**Say goat:** (goat) Change /g/ to /b/. Word?	boat
Say rash: (rash) Change /r/ to /m/. Word?	mash	**Say date:** (date) Change /d/ to /l/. Word?	late
Say mile: (mile) Change /m/ to /p/. Word?	pile	**Say jack:** (jack) Change /j/ to /t/. Word?	tack
Say rag: (rag) Change /r/ to /b/. Word?	bag	**Say pole:** (pole) Change /p/ to /r/. Word?	roll
Say like: (like) Change /l/ to /h/. Word?	hike	**Say seed:** (seed) Change /s/ to /w/. Word?	weed
Say rice: (rice) Change /r/ to /m/. Word?	mice	**Say time:** (time) Change /t/ to /l/. Word?	lime
Say ball: (ball) Change /b/ to /f/. Word?	fall	**Say might:** (might) Change /m/ to /l/. Word?	light
Say too: (too) Change /t/ to /m/. Word?	moo	**Say lock:** (lock) Change /l/ to /r/. Word?	rock